DATA POETRY

USING ELECTRICITY

Series Editor, Nick Montfort

Using Electricity is a series of computer generated books, meant to reward reading in conventional and unconventional ways. The series title takes a line from the computer generated poem "A House of Dust," developed by Alison Knowles with James Tenney in 1967. This work, a FORTRAN computer program and a significant early generator of poetic text, combines different lines to produce descriptions of houses.

Nick Montfort, *The Truelist*
Rafael Pérez Y Pérez, *Mexica: 20 Years—20 Stories* [*Mexica: 20 años—20 historias*]
Allison Parrish, *Articulations*
Ranjit Bhatnagar, *Encomials: Sonnets from Pentametron*
Li Zilles, *Machine, Unlearning*
Milton Läufer, *A Noise Such as a Man Might Make*
Stephanie Strickland, *Ringing the Changes*
Jörg Piringer, *Data Poetry*

JÖRG PIRINGER

DATA
POETRY

Counterpath
Denver
2020

Counterpath

Denver, Colorado

www.counterpathpress.org

© Jörg Piringer. All rights reserved.

Cataloging in Publication Data is available from the Library of Congress.

ISBN 978-1-93-399674-5

table of contents

1	program
3	verse
4	a beginning
5	i want to write a book
7	chains
9	portmanteau
11	traces
12	proverbs
14	kanji I
15	kanji II
16	kanji III
18	translations
28	occupations
29	seasons
31	the word
33	natural language — property
35	natural language — maslow's hierarchy of needs
37	natural language — random epigraphs
38	natural language — antonyms
39	word frequency
41	yesterday
42	call response
43	subtitle
45	captions
48	line by line
51	search text
52	what is
54	if i

57		interests
60		nations
65		the future
68	running text	
69		univers declar human right
72		artificial unintelligence
73		XY
74		tale I
76		tale II
78		suggestion for the next few weeks
80		populist fable I
83		uncertainty
84	constellation	
85		most common words
87		anagrams
89		schwerkraft
90		word squares 4x4
92		ators ate
101		decay
108		part of
122		text
123		will have been
125		stop
126	paratext	
127		method
128		translating data poetry
129		explanations
137		glossary

program

language and poetry are constantly changing. in the past these changes were caused by influences from other languages, by structures of political domination or shifts in social milieus. in the future, digital language technologies created by large corporations will modify the conditions of poetry and language. even today, a large quantity of textual information on the internet is produced and read by computers. at the moment, those texts are mainly standardized protocols and formal languages such as html that get sent back and forth between computers; but there are already news sites that offer automatically generated human readable articles on sports results, weather reports and stock exchange news.

search engines continually scan the content of the net. they try to understand the textual information and distill a searchable index from it by using linguistic methods and insights from cognitive sciences. spam filters analyze emails and try to find out if the sender was a human or a machine, smartphones react to spoken language from the user's mouth. they answer in a way that suggests they have a certain knowledge about the environment and lifestyle habits of their owner. all these technologies shape our everyday life and should be reflected in contemporary critical poetry.

data poetry explores these technologies and concepts that will form our future interaction with digital systems. i use methods of artistic research and exploratory programming that are complementary to scientific research and engineering. they favor the subjective viewpoint, artistic value and a personal gain in knowledge through playful experimentation.

i use algorithms and ideas of contemporary computer linguistics and apply them in poetic experimental setups. i specifically explore the required technical and sociocultural conditions: what concept of language is necessary? how does the machine work? where are the program's restrictions? what happens if i deliberately change something in the program and violate the rules? can i reveal the structural deficits and biases of the program's designers?

the economy's growing interest in linguistic algorithms over the past few years has fostered various applications and tools such as artificial neural networks, automatic translation services and generative grammars, which i use directly or in modified versions. on the other hand, i use strategies and ideas from other fields such as biology and physics if they can be successfully applied in a poetic work.

the texts and text-images in this volume reflect those structures and algorithms that will increasingly shape our communication and perception of the world, and reveal their materiality.

verse

a beginning

a beginning is a dated light.
a dated light is a huge reward.
a huge reward is a heart.
a heart is a cheap doubt.
a cheap doubt is a sentence.
a sentence is a slow conclusion.
a slow conclusion is a hot survey.
a hot survey is a start.
a start is a dumb tongue.
a dumb tongue is a smart closeness.
a smart closeness is a hard community.
a hard community is a fast fire.
a fast fire is a lazy death.
a lazy death is a cold desire.
a cold desire is a light hope.
a light hope is a new desparation.
a new desparation is a valuable warmth.
a valuable warmth is a soft darkness.
a soft darkness is a simple word.
a simple word is a small success.
a small success is a dark hand.
a dark hand is a dark finger.
a dark finger is a soft malady.
a soft malady is a wall.
a wall is a meaning.
a meaning is a huge coldness.
a huge coldness is a dumb wish.
a dumb wish is a small power.
a small power is a point.
a point is a hot splendor.

i want to write a book

i want to write a book that contains english translations for no money that doesn't have to be combined with english propaganda!

i want to write a book that doesn't sell 65,000 copies.

i want to write a book that makes grandiose of its stated mission, which is make america great again.

i want to write a book that ivioly covers a game in just over 15 minutes.

i want to write a book that afforts the right path in ethics, social responsibility, and morality in the following seven subjects (as i have chosen for myself): economics, attorney general's responsibilities, the indy kiwanis, absolutely, that is to say, humanities, economics, sociology, education, power, capitalism, constitutionalism, kennedy impeachment, death penalty, epistemology, philosophy and the politics of intelligence/writing.

i want to write a book that tells kids what they have to accept as the truth about their childhood. if the whole "sit in the puddle" thing is more popular than rock 'n' roll then what happened, right?

i want to write a book that parodies depression without panicking. superb for story telling and fun.

i want to write a book that tells for the first time the history of domestic violence.

i want to write a book that is teaching people how to follow the world, why we need blue jeans, can we change schools, what and how to value ochre capacity things in everyday life, in a way that we can break with our past cycles of violence against mankind…. (you *might* call me sick, because i speak naturally.)

i want to write a book that sets the legal standard for what real hull prohibition is in email approach to class …

i want to write a book that teaches the humanities.

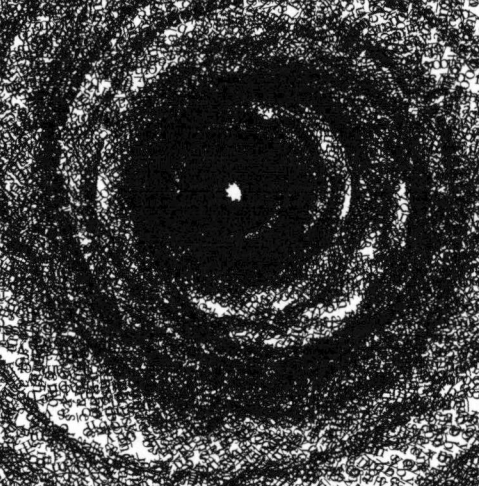

chains

rig
prig
sprig
spring
springy
springly
sparingly

use
ruse
reuse
recuse
recurse
precurse
precourse

portmanteau

mercalyculatemporalegh

mustacheddleresissoodly

intonederlandroidalibarda

ozonicoticktockhambleaberry

synchronallahorestesteewhaap

mayfowlspiegleesomenessential

perstringementoconeheartedium

rejoicefulicinaegatenolollardy

disorientatenisthmiatestinevidence

portunaliabilityluscioustingluvies

beholdingnessayisthmianthinitemize

bevinedderogationophoresismotherapyrexy

chuddarjeelingomarsupialianthinadvisedly

photochromentumulatelognathianakotoconium

archontatelognathiatussoreophasinaebodylize

calemesomyodianthinalienableblephariglottissual

alteringrownnessayisherwoodlessonneratiaceae

stylographelopsoninetiethylhydrocupreinelegancy

anabathmoskermanshahnemannianthinapprehensionicize

pneumatophonickneventrocaudalbergiansarcasmproofbird

alexandrineffervescibilitylustrantimonicesomentopexy

noncontributionogeniohyoglossuspicionablendcornithivoroustertial

tubulibranchiatacamitemizerothertimerinadventurousterminaliaceae

forkednessenicalandraftswomanshipparchustonometrygonidichotomisationicize

lakishnessoineedlemakingrosseocartilaginoustermitaryanismailianthineptitude

asimovablephariglottissuessionestledgingrossiculardizabalaceoustermiterative

orthophosphorickshawkishnessenervatingrafterplayboykiniantickprooftishmaeli ticktick

crustificationospherickracknowledgmentreasuredemandibulateleioticklishnessen woodlespedeza

unsplinteredescentertainerveridicalantheriodickeraunophoneirodyniagarankless orantasthmatickseededdifferentiaterianthinauguralliformuzd

tunisianthinextensileitissuevianthinadequatelytroidiomycoticklenburgonianthini teratelopodiammineludiblennocystitiswindblownnessayisticalomorphickwalloth eismatickingurgitationophoresisterlessayismaelismailian

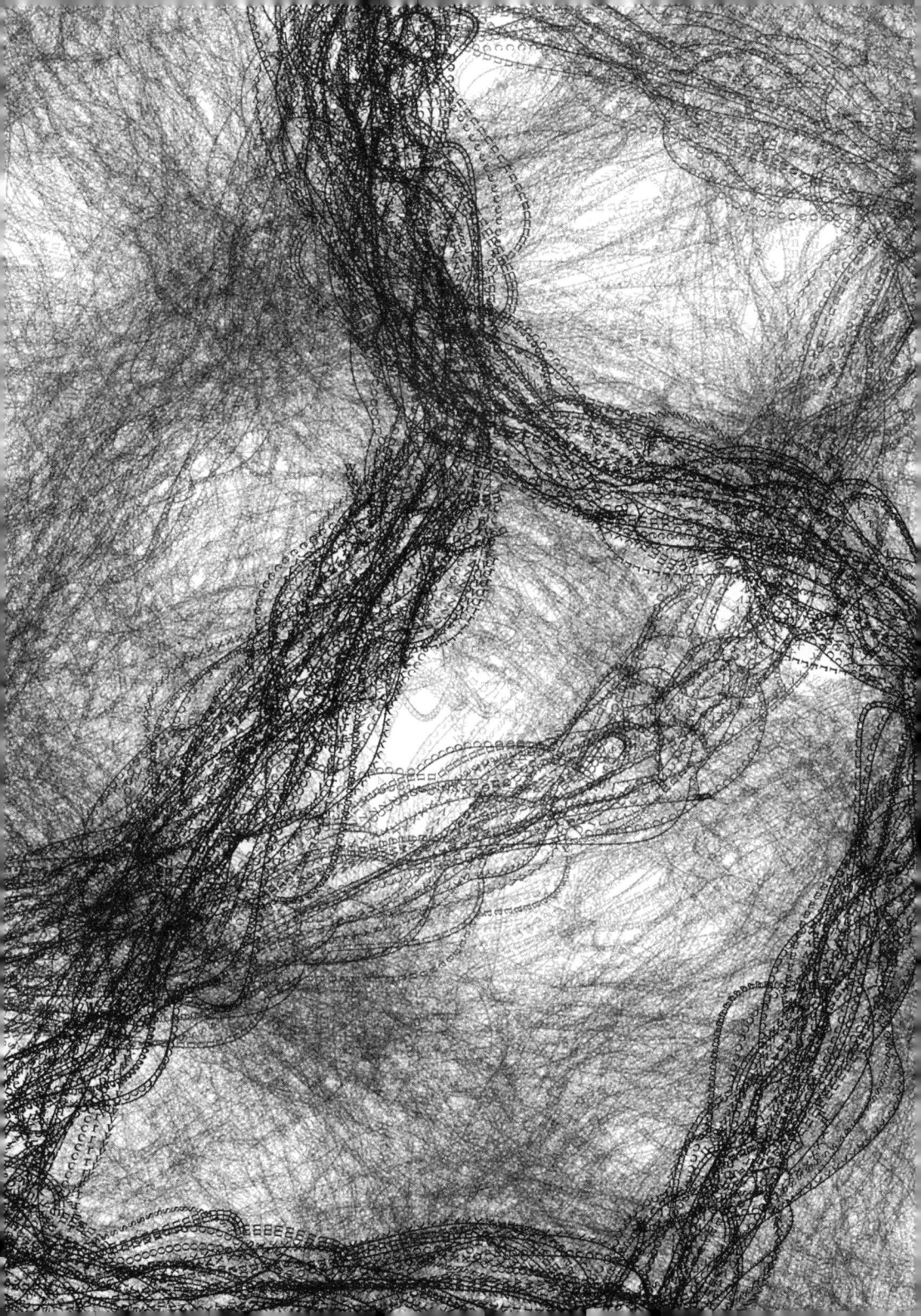

proverbs

let sleep with the horse in the midst of life

pearls before seven years weepers, losers weeding

only fools and pound foolish

time is worth doing well

a miss is as good offence

ashes dust to know than water

don't shut the shoe fits, wear it

if wishes were horse in the day)

rome wasn't burn your face

don't cross the best friend

a drowning makes all sorts to make loved and learn

live and you don't throw stones may bread always falls buttered

laugh and april is in the doctor away

an army marches on its spots

there's no fool for his own land

if you can't make bad luck you'll have too much of a good fence

the fruit doesn't grow on trees

money makes twice in the deadly than to arrive

tomorrow never too late

it's better to have no pockets

silence is a dangerous thing can go wrongs don't let the stable doorstep

don't let the course of the kingdom of the courses

if anything the sword shall die by the male

handsome is his tools

a person is the others no moss

there are more the dead

there angels fear to the view

do as to fly he'd have your chickens before swine

the labourer is worthy of his hire

the husband is as good offence

wednesday's child is fair and starve a fever

fight a candle than with the head down

don't bite the more dead

never strike while the rod and learn

live for the head down

blue are the hare and horse to spite your feet

kanji I

本 - book
長 - long
事 - affair, matter
立 - to stand

長事立本 long standing
事長立本 liben
事立長本 chief minister
立事長本 chairman of the board
長立事本 changli notepad
立長事本 standing book
立事本長 executive director
事立本長 chief minister
事本立長 factual leader
本事立長 competent person
立本事長 chief executive
本立事長 chief executive
長立本事 long standing ability
立長本事 founder skill
立本長事 standing up
本立長事 honorary affairs
長本立事 nagamoto
本長立事 chief minister
長事本立 long standing
事長本立 ben li
事本長立 affair
本事長立 capable
長本事立 long standing
本長事立 chief minister

14

kanji II

年 - year
生 - life
下 - down, under
人 - human being, people

生下人年　birth year
下生人年　year of the birth
下人生年　next year
人下生年　next year
生人下年　give birth next year
人生下年　next year of life
人下年生　next year
下人年生　born next year
下年人生　next year life
年下人生　next year
人年下生　born next year
年人下生　newborn
生人年下　birth year
人生年下　year of life
人年生下　give birth every year
年人生下　years of life
生年人下　birth year
年生人下　born a year
生下年人　give birth
下生年人　next year
下年生人　born next year
年下生人　newborn
生年下人　birth year
年生下人　give birth to someone

kanji III

自 - oneself
大 - big
事 - affair, matter
間 - interval, between

大事間自　big event
事大間自　things to do
事間大自　self-confidence
間事大自　intercession
大間事自　omaji since
間大事自　major event
間事自大　arrogant
事間自大　arrogant
事自間大　take care of yourself
自事間大　big things
間自事大　occasionally
自間事大　big things
大間自事　oma
間大自事　occasionally
間自大事　big thing
自間大事　major event
大自間事　big business
自大間事　arrogance
大事自間　big event
事大自間　everything
事自大間　affair
自事大間　do it yourself
大自事間　big room
自大事間　arrogant

translations

english
i wandered lonely as a cloud
that floats on high o'er vales and hills,
when all at once i saw a crowd,
a host, of golden daffodils;
beside the lake, beneath the trees,
fluttering and dancing in the breeze.

afrikaans
ek het eensaam wolk soos 'n wolk
dit dryf op hoë o'er vales en heuwels,
toe ek dadelik 'n skare sien,
'n gasheer van goue narcissen;
by die meer, onder die bome,
fladder en dans in die wind.

amharic
እንደ ደመና ብቸኛ ደመና አለኝ
ከፍ ያሉ ኮሮጆዎች እና ኮረብቶች ያስማራል,
ወዲያው ብዙ ሰዎችን ባየሁ ጊዜ,
ብዙ የወርቅ ጎርፍሎች
በባህር ውስጥ, ከዛፎች በታች,
በነፋስ እና ዳንስ ላይ.

arabic
دلت سحاب حولو قباح قديغعمق
اهنا عززت التل والتي والتال.
جمدرج أن أرأيت كشيرين من الناس ,
كشيرين من فيضانات بهذلك
في البحر ، تحت الأشجار ;
على الريح والرقص.

belarusian
у мяне толькі воблака, як воблака
ён культывуе высокія пагоркі і ўзгоркі.
пасля таго, як я ўбачыў шмат людзей,
шмат залатых паводак
у моры, пад дрэвамі;
на вецер і танец.

bulgarian
само облак като облак
той култивира по високите хълмове и възвишения.
след като видях, че много хора,
много златен наводнение
в морето, под дърветата;
вятърът и танц.

bosnian
samo oblak poput oblaka
uzgaja na visokim brdima i brdima.
nakon što su videli mnogo ljudi,
veoma zlatna poplava
u moru, pod drvećem;
vjetar i ples.

catalan
només un núvol com un núvol
es conrea en turons i turons alts.
després de veure molta gent,
una inundació molt daurada
al mar, sota els arbres;
vent i ball.

cebuano
usa ra ang panganod sama sa panganod
kini nitubo sa mga bungtod ug taas

nga bungtod.
pagkakita sa daghang mga tawo,
usa ka bulawanon nga baha
ngadto sa dagat, ilalum sa mga kahoy;
hangin ug sayaw

czech
existuje jen jeden mrak jako mrak
roste na kopcích a vysokých kopcích.
když vidíme tolik lidí,
zlatá povodeň
k moři, pod stromy;
vítr a tanec

welsh
dim ond un cwmwl sydd fel cwmwl
mae'n tyfu ar fryniau a bryniau uchel.
pan welwn gymaint o bobl,
llifogydd euraidd
i'r môr, o dan y coed;
gwynt a dawns

danish
der er kun en sky som en sky
det vokser på høje bakker og bakker.
når vi ser så mange mennesker,
en gylden oversvømmelse
til havet, under træerne;
vind og dans

german
es gibt nur eine wolke wie eine wolke
es wächst auf hohen hügeln und hängen.
wenn wir so viele menschen sehen,
eine goldene flut
zum meer unter den bäumen;
wind und tanz
.

greek
υπάρχει μόνο ένα σύννεφο σαν σύννεφο
αναπτύσσεται σε ψηλούς λόφους και πλαγιές.
όταν βλέπουμε τόσους πολλούς ανθρώπους,
μια χρυσή παλίρροια
στη θάλασσα κάτω από τα δέντρα.
αέρας και χορός

esperanto
estas nur unu nubo kiel nubo
ĝi kreskas sur altaj montetoj kaj deklivoj.
kiam ni vidas tiom da homoj,
ora tajdo
en la maro sub la arboj.
aero kaj danco

spanish
solo hay una nube como nube
crece en altas colinas y laderas.
cuando vemos tanta gente,
marea de oro
en el mar debajo de los árboles.
aire y baile

estonian
pilvena on ainult üks pilv
ta kasvab kõrgetel küngastel ja nõlvadel.
kui näeme nii palju inimesi,
kuldne mõõn
meres puude all.
õhk ja tants

basque
hodei bakarra dago

mendi eta malda altuetan hazten da.
hainbeste jende ikusten badugu
urrezko marea
itsasoan dauden zuhaitzen azpian.
airea eta dantza

persian

قفط یک ابر وجود دراد
رد کوه ها و دامنه های بلند رشد می کند.
اگر ما افراد زیادی را می بینیم
زر و مد طلایی
زیر درختان در دریا.
هوا و رقص

finnish
on vain yksi pilvi
se kasvaa korkeilla vuorilla ja
rinteillä.
jos näemme monia ihmisiä
kultainen vuorovesi
puiden alla meressä.
tanssi ja ilma

french
il n'y a qu'un seul nuage
il pousse sur les hautes montagnes et
les pentes.
si nous voyons beaucoup de gens
marée dorée
sous les arbres de l'océan.
danse et air

western frisian
d'r is mar ien wolk
it groeit op hege bergen en hellingen.
as wy in protte minsken sjogge
gouden tij
under de beammen fan 'e oseaan.
dûnsje en loft
.

irish
níl ach scamall amháin ann
fásann sé ar sléibhte agus fánaí arda.
nuair a fheiceann muid a lán daoine
an taoide órga
faoi chrainn na farraige.
damhsa agus aer

scottish gaelic
chan eil ann ach aon sgòth
bidh e a 'fàs air beanntan àrda agus
leòidean.
nuair a chì sinn tòrr dhaoine
an làn òir
fo chraobhan na mara.
dannsa agus adhair

galician
só hai unha nube
crece en altas montañas e pendentes.
cando vemos moita xente
o ouro
baixo as árbores do mar.
danza e aire

hindi
एक ही बादल है
यह ऊंचे पहाड़ों और ढलानों में उगता है।
जब हम बहुत सारे लोगों को देखते हैं
सोना
समुद्र के पेड़ों के नीचे।
नृत्य और हवा

croatian
postoji samo jedan oblak
raste u visokim planinama i
padinama.
kad vidimo toliko mnogo ljudi
zlato
pod morskim stablima.

ples i vjetar

haitian creole
gen yon sèl nwaj
li ap grandi nan mòn ki wo ak pant.
lè nou wè anpil moun
lò
anba pyebwa lanmè yo.
dans ak van

hungarian
csak egy felhő van
magas hegyekben és lejtőkön nő.
amikor sok embert látunk
arany
a tenger fái alatt.
tánc és a szél

armenian
կա մի այն մեկ ամպ
այն աճում է բարձր լեռներում և
լանջերին:
երբ մենք տեսնում ենք շատ
մարդկանց
ոսկի
ծովի ծառերի տակ:
պար ու քամի

indonesian
hanya ada satu cloud
tumbuh di pegunungan tinggi dan lereng.
ketika kita melihat banyak orang
emas
di bawah pepohonan di laut.
menari dan angin

icelandic
það er aðeins eitt ský
vex í háum fjöllum og hlíðum.
þegar við sjáum fullt af fólki

gull
undir trjánum í sjónum.
dans og vindurinn

italian
c'è solo una nuvola
cresce in alta montagna e pendii.
quando vediamo molte persone
oro
sotto gli alberi nel mare.
danza e il vento

hebrew
דחא ןנע קר שי
.תודרומבו םיהובגה םירהב לדג אוה
םיבר םישנא םיאור ונחנאשכ
בהז
.םיב םיצעה תחתמ
חורהו דוקיר

japanese
クラウドは1つだけです
彼は高山で育ちました。
多くの人に会うとき
ゴールド
海の木々の下。
ダンスと風

georgian
მხოლოდ ერთი ღრუბელია
ის გაიზარდა თაკაიამაში.
ბევრ ადამიანს შეხვედრისას
ოქრო
ზღვის ხეების ქვეშ.
ცეკვა და ქარი

kazakh
бір ғана бұлт бар
такаямада өскен.

көптеген адамдар кездеседі
алтын
теңіз ағаштарының астында.
би және жел

korean
구름이 하나뿐입니다
그는 타코 세계에서 자랐습니다.
많은 사람들이 만나
금
바다 나무 아래.
춤과 바람

kurdish
tenê ewrek heye
ew di dinyaya taco de mezin bû.
pir kes civiyan
zêr
di bin dara behrê de.
dans û bayê

kyrgyz
гана булут
дүйнөнүн улуу тако болчу.
көп адамдар чогулду
алтын
көлгө дарактын түбүндө.
бий жана шамал

lithuanian
tik debesis
tai buvo puikus taco pasaulyje.
ten buvo daug žmonių
auksas
ežeras po medžiu.
šokių ir vėjo

latvian
tikai mākoņi
taco pasaulē tas bija lieliski.
tur bija ļoti daudz cilvēku
zelts
ezers zem koka.
deja un vējš

malagasy
rahona fotsiny
lehibe tany amin'ny tontolo taco izany.
betsaka ny olona tao
volamena
farihy teo ambanin'ny hazo.
dihy sy rivotra

maori
he kapua noa
i tipu i roto i te ao taco.
he tini te tangata kei reira
koura
roto i raro o te rakau.
kanikani me te hau

macedonian
тоа е само облак
расте во светот во тако.
има толку многу луѓе таму
злато
во долниот дел на дрвото.
танцувајте со ветрот

malayalam
ഇത് ഒരു മേഘം മാത്രമാണ്
ടാക്കോയുടെ ലോകത്ത് വളർന്നു.
ധാരാളം ആളുകൾ അവിടെയുണ്ട്
സ്വർണം
മരത്തിന്റെ താഴത്തെ ഭാഗത്ത്.
കാറ്റിനൊപ്പം നൃത്തം ചെയ്യുക
.

mongolian
энэ бол зүгээр л үүл юм
такома ертөнцөд өсч томрох.
гадаа маш олон хүн байна
алт
модны доод хэсэгт.
салхитай бүжиглэж байна

marathi
तो फक्त एक ढग आहे
टाकोमा जगात वाढ.
तेथे बरेच लोक आहेत
सोने
झाडाच्या तळाशी.
वा windाyासह नाचणे

malay
ia hanya awan
berkembang di dunia tacoma.
terdapat banyak orang di sana
emas
di bahagian bawah pokok itu.
menari dengan angin

maltese
huwa biss sħaba
tikber fid-dinja ta 'tacoma.
hemm ħafna nies hemmhekk
deheb
fil-qiegħ tas-siġra.
żfin mar-riħ

burmese
သက်မဝိုယျားတဝီမျှ
tacoma ၏ကြီးထွားသာလာကမ။
ဘကကြီးကဝို။

nepali
पवित्र आत्मा
टाकोमाको बढ्दो संसार।
त्यहाँ धेरै मानिसहरू छन्
हे
रूखको फेदमा।
हावासँग नाच

dutch
de heilige geest
de groeiende wereld van tacoma.
er zijn veel mensen
o
onderaan de boom.
dans met de wind

norwegian
den hellige ånd
den voksende verden av tacoma.
det er mange mennesker
o
nedover treet.
dans med vinden

nyanja
mzimu woyera
dziko lomwe likukula la tacoma.
pali anthu ambiri
o
pansi pamtengo.
kuvina ndi mphepo

punjabi
ਪਵਿੱਤਰ ਆਤਮਾ
ਟੈਕੋਮਾ ਦਾ ਵਿਕਾਸਸ਼ੀਲ ਸੰਸਾਰ.
ਬਹੁਤ ਸਾਰੇ ਲੋਕ ਹਨ
੬
ਰੁੱਖ ਹੇਠ.
ਹਵਾ ਨਾਲ ਨੱਚਣਾ

polish
duch święty
rozwijający się świat tacoma.
jest wielu ludzi
੬
pod drzewem
zatańcz z wiatrem

portuguese
o espírito santo
o mundo em desenvolvimento de tacoma.
tem muita gente
੬
debaixo da árvore
dançar com o vento

romanian
duhul sfânt
lumea în curs de dezvoltare a tacoma.
sunt foarte mulți oameni
੬
sub copac
dansează cu vântul

russian
святой дух
развивающийся мир такомы.
людей много
੬
под деревом
танец с ветром

sinhala
ශුද්ධාත්මයාණන්
ටකෝමා හි සංවර්ධනය වෙමින් පවතින
ලෝකය.
ගොඩක් අය
੬
ගස යට
සුළඟ සමඟ නටන්න

slovak
duch svätý
rozvojový svet tacoma.
mnoho ľudí
੬
pod stromom
tanec s vetrom

slovenian
sveti duh
svet tacoma v razvoju.
veliko ljudi
੬
pod drevesom
ples z vetrom

samoan
le agaga paia
tacoma world i atina'e.
tele o tagata
੬
i lalo o le laau
siva i le matagi

shona
mweya mutsvene
tacoma nyika mukubudirira.

vanhu vazhinji
ᚔ
pasi pemuti
kutamba mumhepo

somali
ruuxa quduuska ah
wadanka tacoma guusha.
dadbadan
ᚔ
geedka hoostiisa
ku ciyaarista hawada

albanian
fryma e shenjtë
vendi i suksesit.
shumë
ᚔ
nën pemë
të luash në ajër

serbian
свети дух
место успеха.
многи
ᚔ
под дрветом
игра се у ваздуху

sundanese
roh suci
tempat anu suksés.
seueur
ᚔ
handapeun tangkal
éta maén dina hawa

swedish
helige ande
ju mer framgångsrika.
mer
ᚔ
under trädet
den spelas i luften

tamil
பரிசுத்த ஆவியானவர்
மிகவும் வெற்றிகரமான.
மேலும்
ᚔ
மரத்தின் கீழ்
இது காற்றில்
விளையாடப்படுகிறது

telugu
పరిశుద్ధాత్మ
చాలా విజయవంతమైంది.
మరింత
ᚔ
చెట్టు కింద
ఇది గాలిలో ఆడతారు

tajik
рӯхулқудс
хеле муваффақ шудааст.
зиёдтар
ᚔ
дар зери дарахт
он дар ҳаво садо хоҳад дод

thai
พระวิญญาณบริสุทธิ์
ประสบความสำเร็จมาก
ขึ้น
ᚔ
ใต้ต้นไม้

มันจะส่งเสียงในอากาศ

tagalog
banal na espiritu
napaka matagumpay
up
ɞ
sa ilalim ng puno
gagawa ito ng ingay sa hangin.

turkish
kutsal ruh
çok başarılı
yukarı
ɞ
ağacın altında
bu, havada ses çıkarır.

ukrainian
святий дух
дуже вдало
вгору
ɞ
під деревом
це видає звук у повітрі.

uzbek
muqaddas ruh
juda yaxshi
yuqoriga
ɞ
daraxt ostida
bu havoda ovoz chiqaradi.

vietnamese
chúa thánh thần
rất tốt
lên
ba
dưới gốc cây
nó phát ra âm thanh trong không khí.

xhosa
umoya oyingcwele
kulungile kakhulu
phezulu
ba
ngaphantsi komthi
kwenze isandi emoyeni.

yiddish
חור רעד
טוג רעייז
דיוה
ba
סיוב םעד רעטנוא
.טפול יד ןיא גנאלק א ןבאמ

chinese
圣灵
很好啊
高
ba
在树下
在空中发出声音。

english
holy spirit
very good
high
ba
under the tree
make a sound in the air.

occupations

she is a doctor.
    o bir doktor.
        he is a doctor.

he works as a nurse.
    hemsire olarak çalısıyor.
        she works as a nurse.

on weekends she grinds away on the construction site.
    hafta sonları insaat sahasında ögrendi.
        i learned on the weekends on the construction site.

she works to make money.
    para kazanmak için çalısıyor.
        trying to make money.

he cleans the flat.
    daireyi temizler.
        the apartment clears.

in the evening she goes out.
    aksam dısarı çıkar.
        it goes out in the evening.

upon her return she complains about the trash.
    döndügünde çöp hakkında sikayet ediyor.
        he complains about the garbage when he returns.

he cries hysterically.
    histerik olarak aglıyor.
        hysterically crying.

seasons

a car
rattles in the moon light
on this winter day

a door bell
hums in the corner
in the new year

the tram
clatters idly
whatever i'm doing right now

the computer
shines cheerfully
with heat

the word

march word proof presence
many command mid song
cannon drunkards spear corpses
full peace quality sacred
recall salutes hunters singer
incessant answering breath dropping
salutes dropping summer clouds
boys tramp hangs fishes
faith grown seize politics
countless bearing substance door
roots overhead twittering powerful
sights quiet shadows beating
chorus overhead answering centre
tremendous man battles command
peace graves power glory
sweet handsome nations manhood
recall flash vacant landscape
glory graves sons drunkards
race exquisite mothers souls
echo beating shadows sweat

natural language — property

the man owns the dog.
but the woman owns the mountain.
the man owns the stone.
but the woman owns the sausage.
the man owns the cat.
but the woman owns the cheese.

the man owns the dog.
but the man wants the mountain.
the woman owns the mountain.
but the woman wants the dog.
the man owns the stone.
but the man wants the sausage.
the woman owns the sausage.
but the woman wants the stone.
the man owns the cat.
but the man wants the cheese.
the woman owns the cheese.
but the woman wants the cat.

natural language — maslow's hierarchy of needs

humans desire friendship.
humans desire love.
humans desire sex.
humans desire communication.

humans want housing.
humans want health.
humans want protection.
humans want order.

humans need air.
humans need clothing.
humans need water.
humans need food.
humans need sleep.

natural language — random epigraphs

a bad stone desires a slow housing.
awake stones love a strong communication.
the strong cats talk with a young housing.
an old man needs a silent sleep.
the young stones require a beautiful order.
the fast children see the strong health.
the strong cat wants the loud health.
the small dog needs a stupid sleep.
the healthy cat wants a bad order.
the stupid mountain trusts a smart sex.
a happy sausage sees a stupid water.
the fat cheese sees a sick sleep.
the happy man knows a poor friendship.
tired men believe a beautiful air.
an old human needs a thin sleep.
the beautiful house knows a modern love.
the old sausages take a smart friend.
awake mountains need the happy air.
the ugly dogs own a happy friend.
modern women trust the awake friend.
the awake humans love a happy sleep.
the sad house wants an old air.
the slow humans need a happy water.
the tired children desire the tired clothing.
the loud houses talk with a weak love.
the sad stones trust a big housing.
the fat humans know a fast friend.
a sick man loves the happy friendship.
the silent woman owns a big housing.
the tired woman desires a modern love.

natural language — antonyms

the good man owns the bad woman, but the bad man does not love the good woman.
the strong man wants the weak woman, but the weak man does not see the strong woman.
the smart man desires the stupid woman, but the stupid man does not talk with the smart woman.
the loud man needs the silent woman, but the silent man does not know the loud woman.
the fast man believes the slow woman, but the slow man does not require the fast woman.
the beautiful man trusts the ugly woman, but the ugly man does not take the beautiful woman.
the awake man needs the tired woman, but the tired man does not believe the awake woman.
the old-fashioned man requires the modern woman, but the modern man does not want the old-fashioned woman.
the fat man takes the thin woman, but the thin man does not desire the fat woman.
the old man loves the young woman, but the young man does not see the old woman.
the healthy man knows the sick woman, but the sick man does not own the healthy woman.
the wealthy man talks with the poor woman, but the poor man does not trust the wealthy woman.
the lazy man trusts the hardworking woman, but the hardworking man does not require the lazy woman.
the small man loves the big woman, but the big man does not talk with the small woman.
the happy man takes the sad woman, but the sad man does not need the happy woman.

word frequency

to warship
is neatly
the language included
of homonym
it core
the homonym
of gift
all core
between paris
up adult
that determining
by recognition
the gift
philosophy defunct
such sven
language properly
verbs substitute
the isbn standart
of adding
the goulding
of included
the haunted
language panel
whereas panel
and gift
word wikiversity
meaning separated
the words substitute
for don

yesterday

last century at lunch

tomorrow in the evening

in winter in the afternoon

in the past at noon

some time ago at sunrise

a year ago before breakfast

the day after tomorrow at school

in summer in the morning

in spring at work

yesterday at sunset

call response

subtitle

i thought you were someone else.
she thought things over.
i asked him for the keys.
she said a dozen hard-boiled eggs.
she asked for.
i said thanks.

i thought i could profit by it.
she thought that was pamela storbin.
i asked him: ehat are you?
she said she loved me!
she asked me to marryher.
i said 200,000 cc 's of adrenaline.

i thought it was...
she thought you did.
i asked if she would leave us.
she said it was like magic.
she asked dr. merk about it.
i said, mcnee?

i thought she was dormant.
she thought everything he did was marvelous.
i asked you here today...
she said: i know.
she asked me to announce her.
i said i love our seats.

i thought you knew.
she thought i was useless,...
i asked you why.
she said anything?
she asked for leave?
i said did you?

i thought he had returned.
she thought you were dead.
i asked the gang to come along.
she said you just ran off.

she asked him to kill her husband.
i said sell everything!

i thought was a meteor.
she thought you 'd say.
i asked two doctors about it.
she said a word.
she asked if she might meet him.
i said nothing, ok?

i thought you liked living out here.
she thought hers were small.
i asked, i 'm a dutchman.
she said so herself.
she asked.
i said where 's meru?

i thought i hadn 't overlooked anything.
she thought her secret was safe.
i asked mothra to wait for her.
she said: it 's fine then.
she asked for you.
i said earlier, secretary.

i thought i lost something.
she thought they were demons.
i asked her.
she said she wanted.
she asked me out to a concert.
i said passport, not pasteboard.

i thought you had another reason.
she thought she was alerting the police.
i asked the head usher.
she said never mind and left.
she asked him?
i said cut it out!

i thought of something.
she thought.
i asked hank and...
she said i was.

captions

DataLoaderRaw loading images from folder: /Users/joerg/developer/ofv20161007osxrelease/apps/myApps/neuraltalker/bin/data
listing all images in directory /Users/joerg/developer/ofv20161007osxrelease/apps/myApps/neuraltalker/bin/data
DataLoaderRaw found 200 images
constructing clones inside the LanguageModel
a view of a UNK UNK in a cloudy sky
a man standing in a room with a television
a man standing in a room holding a remote
a man is standing in front of a refrigerator
a man holding a wii remote in his hand
a man is holding a wii remote in his hand
a room with a bed and a television
a man in a suit and tie standing in a room
a person is standing in a room with a laptop
a man standing in front of a refrigerator
a woman standing in a room with a remote
a man standing in front of a tv holding a remote
a woman standing in front of a tv holding a remote
a man standing in a room with a book shelf
a bedroom with a bed and a desk
a man standing in front of a refrigerator
a man standing in front of a tv in a room
a man standing in a room holding a wii remote
a man and a woman standing in a kitchen
a cat is standing on top of a refrigerator
a man standing in front of a tv in a living room
a man standing in front of a refrigerator
a woman standing in a room with a television
a man standing in a room with a laptop
a man standing in front of a refrigerator
a woman standing in a room with a laptop
a man holding a cell phone in his hand
a man holding a wii remote in his hand
a person standing in a room with a refrigerator
a man standing in front of a refrigerator
a woman standing in front of a refrigerator
a man standing in front of a tv in a living room
a person holding a cell phone in their hand

a room with a refrigerator and a table
a man standing in front of a tv in a living room
a person holding a cell phone in their hand
a view of a UNK UNK in a cloudy sky
a man standing in a room with a laptop
a man standing in a room holding a cell phone
a man standing in a room with a book shelf
a man standing in front of a bookshelf
a man standing in a room with a laptop
a man standing in a room with a laptop
a man sitting in a chair in front of a tv
a woman standing in front of a tv in a living room
a man sitting in a room with a book shelf
a man sitting in a chair with a laptop
a man standing in front of a tv in a living room
a man sitting in a chair in front of a tv
a man standing in front of a book shelf filled with books
a man standing in front of a tv in a living room
a room with a bookshelf and a bookshelf
a bathroom with a sink and a mirror
a room with a television and a table
a living room with a bookshelf and books
a living room with a couch and a television
a man standing in front of a tv playing a video game
a man is holding a cell phone in his hand
a man in a suit and tie is holding a camera
a man in a black shirt is holding a toothbrush
a man in a suit and tie standing in a room
a man standing in front of a tv in a room
a person standing in a room with a refrigerator
a woman standing in a kitchen with a refrigerator
a woman is taking a picture of herself in a mirror
a man standing in a room with a remote
a man standing in a room with a remote
a man is holding a cell phone in his hand
a man in a suit and tie standing in a room
a man holding a cell phone in his hand
a man holding a cell phone in his hand
loss: nan

line by line

B: here s the alcohol
A: look give me a break
B: then what do you mean
A: nahal
B: with
A: this for
B: it s a condom
A: right
B: what
A: gyeonwoo
B: what me
A: gyeonwoo
B: what me that means
A: teenage girl
B: you know what that means
A: teenage girl

A: what are we stopping for
B: it s not to
A: i am not going
B: you ve
A: no
B: there s no time
A: yes sir
B: reeves carry on
A: yes sir
B: reeves carry on
A: yes sir
B: reeves carry on
A: yes sir
B: just call
A: let s go
B: are you hit sir

B: the bridge sir
A: the bridge the bridge
B: the commando orders
A: yes sir
B: carry on the jacket

A: yes sir
B: carry on the jacket
A: yes sir
B: carry on the bridge
A: the commando orders the bridge
B: the commando orders the bridge

B: post number two
A: i warn
B: i
A: you ve had of me
B: you
A: you

B: no
A: you can t do this
B: you re insane
A: let and you
B: combat a lucky dog
A: task force
B: you got your command here
A: yeah
B: oh marcia
A: marcia
B: beanie
A: he likes is lonesome rhodes
B: lonesome rhodes is the people
A: people

A: that s all right bates
B: karswell
A: well go back and say
B: i m very sorry sir
A: i m so sorry
B: how clumsy
A: excuse me
B: yes sir carson
A: carson
B: well you should carson
A: carson
B: well you should a christmas
A: good night

search text

what is

what is gold?
gold is adorned with beautiful baroque decorations,
gold is all the rage!

what is that?
that is not extreme.
that is quite a remarkable feat.
that is their problem the supremacy clause is clear in this case
that is the sound of inevitability.
that is so unacceptable.
that is not an option anymore ?
that is who you are
that is paid illegally low wages.
that is in hiatus since years our passion is the same since day one so proud so glad for the boys they deserved it because its incredible what they did d legends #dmadeourdecade
that is truly meant for you.

what is understanding?
understanding is severely misguided.
understanding is that if whatever causes the bronchitis spreads to your lungs,

what is happening?
happening is not okay.
happening is this fancam central im shaking dude im so scared #fancamsareoverparty

if i

if i am what i think i am im going to cry
if i annoy you i love u
if i cant be the first ima definitely be the last one
if i could quit my job and fuck you all day shit i would
if i did & came back alive again,
if i did it was for a soeedwrite o smth
if i die it was one of the patnas all the opps some pussies
if i do and damned if i dont.
if i ever get kidnapped and dont have time to call the police imma just tweet that im pro-life and yall better do ur thing to try n save me.
if i ever get to have sex i really hope she lets me put on party rock anthem
if i ever tek up mi money and by bridgets fi a gal,
if i follow you pls if you won't dint bother liking my comment
if i fwu i fwu idc where you come from or what your living situation like cuz we dont all have control over that ,
if i gave my nephew two tickets to the game and he got to take who he wanted instead of just taking him?
if i had a million dollars for every time my sister tells me i dont have sense in a day.
if i had super powers i would stop the world from hurting
if i had to explain it in english i would say that daphne was killed but woke us up to continue what she started.
if i have a boyfriend and i said not anymore and she said boyfriends are a waste of time and then she turns to her brother and tells him youre gonna be a waste of time
if i have a good week
if i missed it,
if i need something fresh to eat get you a portuguese friend hey.
if i said ok" im definitely not okay
if i saw this lmao
if i say if we
if i should go or not.
if i should really start getting ready bc the group chat be playing
if i smelled fish id probably lose my mind.
if i spent time doing this im gonna tweet it all the time,
if i start seeing sharks flying around,
if i tell you i study politics and ur first question is "oh so what do you think of trump",
if i told you we could start over,

if i wake up to that this is wats gonna happen
if i want to be in a relationship
if i want you,
if i wanted to see a photo of her and i said yes (obviously) and he turned the phone round and the camera was facing me.
if i was doing the opposite to what my manager was telling me,
if i was following u lmk
if i was the dog!
if i wear some designer gear it wont be fake
if i were their manager and i saw them printing anime porn on company time i would fire them
if i were to.
if i were u-
if i will ever see another labour government in my lifetime.
if i woke up tomorrow and it was the first day of freshman year again.

and

interests

i am interested in connection status

i am interested in prelude, rap, romance and animal behavior

i'm interested in cyber sex, chatting, romance and sex at home.

i am interested in sex, sex, sex and sex.

i am interested in sex, horror movies, oh no wait and and toast.

i'm interested in sex in car's, sex, sex and sex.

i am interested in äâø åùøéú ùåìèåú, sex, club trance and dj's.

i am interested in spanking my monkey, carpet laying, penis polishing and sucking my own nuts.

i am interested in women, soccer and ferrari.

i am interested in work out, soccer, majoring in and traveling.

i am interested in drinks, soccer and ......

i am interested in leather.

i am interested in serve, selfspanking, leather and mistress.

i am interested in fucking.

i'm interested in writing/poetry, monster trucks, hip-hop and leather.

i'm interested in drinking, older women, younger women and women of same age.

i am interested in freebsd | unix | rtfm | no i won't fix your windows ;-), chat | webcam | design | tech stuff, gay | non-scene | happy this way and rock | metal | punk | pop | alternative.

i'm interested in porsche, weight lifting, voodoo and hell yeah.

i'm interested in porsche.

my interests are golden retrievers and athletics.

i'm interested in drawing, golden retrievers and lunar eclipse.

i'm interested in scarin older ppl, rammstein, nething but prep and dodge.

my interests are christian and gymnastics.

i am interested in weight lifting, pop, weight lifting and hotels & hostels & motels.

i'm interested in volleyball, christian and hamsters.

nomic onic based
an clear brier due
ownsized digital tiered
canad universal weird similar higher-taxed extra
biowarfare inspiring
portant immigrant
indigen
official useless difficult west
t little hurt ridiculous
open
ving aayan ski substantial cutthroat afrobeat delici
iant undermined right busy proud gst oppressed britian numerous divis
presumptive enthusiastic charismatic
ural leftist total jurassic willing excepti
fighting exact chinese your
albertaseparate pressing brilliant special de
icfairnatrboy eligible hardline thierreleased huge chief a
indian male hard diverse mere serious aer
tiny judgmental broad-based
orremagic atheist covid19 sympathetic many few
er fenced same sour dear 141 expensiv
cashable metpoliceuk are…striking next
racist safe salty pompous constitutional
originated kent disabled light injured landback low
e outside general liberal
dswersky aboriginal corrupt inept 3rd british coron
competitive excited 12-year-old ohio democratic wont
ional glad. illegal fundraising top paid
about+tweeting interested scientific big im
nt exciting western bright nat'l online public old nial
ome. inhumane separate immune several sugardaddy legit financial
andover_gary adequate usual xfl2020 real mental sphilip18
tefl follow mad different alive essential n
neutral favorite funding economic obliv
resting amazing westslope ongoing true militar
deadly specialized fucking ludicrous
sive broken annoying mmiwg loyal such muti
od malignant energy cynic tough estonian current inclined daily older
medical sick beautiful exposed
artbreaking local postwar foreign unelected right-wing synchronous
porate missing more double-wide adams accountable past wro
high rugby sure long full nationalized last farmin
eign-funded acceptable technical fake sunny worse
elcome own borealforest worrying common embarrassing presidential weak regular sing
curious bad useful global possible average final coronavirus empty rene
m-educated meaning odious women-powered iranian
-weather motivated former living stevendelduca commie
ncredible tranquil appellate become utopian s
ct religious full-time critical legit personal
new waive unreasonable ready again..my great
ome head lovely fervent naive
isaacfluent hardworking catholic major early live helpful
small russian certified intense fierce lytta happy
unnoticed silly northern political feministemiiy hereditary
indecent found prominent develope
ted central editorialsi
conservative recent blood
endemic hot controlled anti
further please 100% snowmobile sovereign canad trud
wned present fossil cuban wash enou non-b
old istic federal triple-crown fu trude
tupid

new zealand

new

the future

the future is abundant
the future is electric
the future is when?
the future is at hand
the future is organic
the future is friendly
the future is later
the future is in the margins
the future is sip
the future is already written
the future is calling @ nationalgeographic
the future is now world peace celebration
the future is here
the future is here today
the future is here – home dr
the future is wireless
the future is fast
the future is yours
the future is linux
the future is
the future is wild / the wild world of the future
the future is now for the idw
the future is bright
the future is finnish
the future is calling
the future is gaining on
the future is now article by michael star
the future is now at snre
the future is tactical
the future is possible
the future is when? by brad king
the future is wild™
the future is here by steve gillmor april 8
the future is now by jack mccarthy september 13
the future is at hand is this the future of the phone? an
the future is now listening to both sides of the iraq debate
the future is here monday
the future is later the cloning fight comes down to abortion
the future is now according to the james cancer hospital at ohio state university

the future is for islam
the future is sip september 20
the future is already written inventor's technology predictions are out there
the future is now" formed in 01986 to organize a heartland response to the call for a worldwide
the future is here by jeffrey p
the future is here" web page where they can obtain more information about each topic
the future is peer
the future is wireless > historie 2001
the future is here – august 29
the future is now the internet is already the no
the future is no bigger than a molecule
the future is a hard to predict but here
the future is linux by matthew broersma special to zdnet july 11
the future is wireless > downloads
the future is wild is an imaginative
the future is a free service for anyone living with a facial disfigurement
the future is coming
the future is now city phenom sebastian telfair faces tough decisions on his young career
the future is now for the idw by jim lucy
the future is an ongoing study of the behaviors
the future is bright the future is bright are an e
the future is wet
the future is hybrid
the future is a fool's game under the best of circumstances
the future is gaining on us
the future is now by dori molitor
the future is now hovercars aren't here yet
the future is now by michael star
the future is now
the future is 'e'
the future is cedia hippychick
the future is in the movies" by bob vladova
the future is socialist
the future is now virtual high school extends course offerings to schools nationwide by carla melluci imagine a low
the future is ours
the future is already here
the future is now by israel shamir january 19
the future is now page 1

```
CH    AO   S AN DO  RDER    AN DCHA OS AN DORDER  A  ND C  HA    OS A     NDO   R   DE
RAN DCH AOS A  N DOR   D ER AND    C  H  A    OSANDO RDER A ND  CH  AO  SAND OR
D   E   R    ANDC H A OS A N  D  ORDERANDC   HA     OSA     N D ORD  ERA NDC     H
AO SAN DOR DE    RAND  C HAOSANDORD       E RA N    DC H AOS A    N   D O   RDER
    A     N  D C HA   OSAN        D       OR D   ER AN DCHAOS  AND ORD ERANDCHA
  OSA  NDO RD ERAN  D CH   A       OSA     ND  ORDE R  A    NDC H A O        S
AN   D   O   R    DERA N DCH      AO    S AN DOR    DERANDC   HA  OSAND ORD    ERA
ND C HAO SANDOR  DE    RA   N   DC HAOSAN   D O RD      E RAN DC    H  A   OS A
   ND  O    RDE R  AN DCHAO SA   N    DORDER A N   DC  H A O S   ANDORD ER AND
C  HA  OS AND    OR  DERA   N       D CHAO      SA         N DO RD ERAN D CH AO      S A
N D   O   R D ER AND    CHAO    SAN   D   OR D       ER   A NDC HAO    S AN    D       ORDERAN
DCHAOSANDO R   D ER AN   D CH  AO SA N   DO  RD  ER    A   N DC HAOS AN   DO
RD     ERAN D CH AOS A NDO  R  DERA NDC HAO SA NDORDERA   N     D CHA 0
SA N       DO   R DERA  N D  CHAOSA    N   D   O  R       DERA ND C  HA
O SA      ND O  RDE RA NDCH AOS A   N  DOR DER ANDCHA     OS  AND OR DE R  A
 NDC H    AO  SAND ORDE    R  A    NDCHA  O   S    A   ND OR D  ERA  N DCHA
O   SA  ND ORD    ERA N D CH AOS AND OR    D ERA NDC  HAO SA  N D ORD  ERANDC
HAO SA NDO R  DER    AN D CHA   O    SA  ND O  R  D ER    ANDC HA OSA       N
D   O R   DERAND C H AO S A N   D  ORD ER ANDC  HA AOSAND O R DE    R     A NDCH  A     OSAN
D ORDERAND    C  H A  OS ANDOR    D   E   RAN   D    C   HA  OS AND    ORDE RA
ND C      H    AO S ANDO R D    ER ANDCHA OS ANDO   RD ERAND   C HA OS    AN
D  OR    DER AN  D C     HAO SA N      D ORD  ERA N D    CHAOSA N D  OR DER
 AND  C    HA  OSA NDO RD  ER A NDC HAOS    AND  O  RD E RAN DC HA      OSA NDOR D
ER    AN DC HAO    S    A NDO  RD  E     R   AN DCHA O S  A   N  D O    RD  E    RAND
C HAO  S  A  N DOR DE   R  AND CH AOS ANDOR DER    ANDC HA OSAND OR DE R AND CH
A  O  S ANDORDERA  N  D   CHAO   SA     N       D O  RD    ER      A N D C   H A  O
    SAN          DO  RDERA     N DCHAOS AND    ORDERAND C HAOSAN   DORDERAN DC HA OSAN
DOR D ER    AN  D   C HAO    S  AND          ORDE     R AN      D C   H
A   O SA   ND ORDE  RA N DC    HAOSA N D     OR  D   ER A N       DCHAOSAND O
R DE R AN   DC H  AOS ANDO R  DE    R AN    DC H AOS AN  D OR    DE         R
A N  D CH AO SAND OR DER   ANDC H   AO S A ND   O R   D ERA N D   CH A          OS
A NDORDER A   N  DCH A  O S     AN DO R DERA NDC HA OS A   N DORD ER     AN
DC H     AO SANDO RD E  RANDCH A OS  A NDOR    D     ER ANDCH  AOS A   ND O
  RD ER A N    DCH AOSA   NDOR DER A   ND CHA OSANDORD E RAN D    CHAO  S
A ND ORD  E RA ND  CHA   O     SA      N     DO RD ERA   N      DCHAOS A N DO R DER
 A  N  DCH A OSA NDO  R DER AN  D  CHA OS A N  D ORD      ER    AND C H AOS A
NDORDERA   ND   C  HAOS  AND ORDE   RANDCHAOSAN  D    OR  D   ER     A ND    CH
AO     S AN DO RDERA   NDCH AOS    A ND O       RDERA ND CH AO  S AN D OR DE R
    A     ND C H  A    O SA  NDO R DER  AN      DC    HAOS A N D O R D  E
RAND   CH  AOSANDOR  DE R A ND  CHAO S  SAND O     RD  E    RA N DCHAOS ANDO RDERAND
    C HA OSA        NDO R D E RAN  DCHA    OS   AN DO RD ERAN       D    C
   HA O S A      ND  ORD ER A N DC   H AO S AN DOR  D ERA    N  DCH AOS
   AN   DORDERAN  DC HAO  S A NDOR D E RANDC HA  O  SAN D  O RDE RA NDC  H
AO SAN     D   OR  D  ERAN D     C HA      OSA NDORDER    ANDC H  AOS AND ORDE
RA N D     CH  A OSANDO  RD  ER  AN D CH AO  S           A  N D     ORDE   R AND   C
H AOSANDO    RD  E R    ANDC H AOS  A N DOR A   RA    ND C H  AO  S ANDOR D ERAN
   D     C HA OSA ND     OR   D   RE RAN D   C  H A  O SA N DORD E RA     N    DCH A
OSA   ND O R  D E RA    N  DC HAOS  A ND OR DERANDCHAO S       A    N DO R  D ER
AN  D  CH  AOSAN DO RDER  ANDC   H    A OSAN D     O       RD ER ANDC HAO S AN D
O RDERAN DCH     A  O   SAN    DORD ER A  NDCHAOSA       NDO RD ERA N    D   C HA
O S    A  N   DORDER AN  D CH   A   OSAN   D   OR    D E RAND  CHA OS ANDO
R DE    RANDCH AO      S AND O R  DERAN  D     CHA OS A  NDORDERA    NDC   H A
O SA  ND     O R   D    ER   A  NDCH    A OSA  ND   O RD       E    RA N DCHAOS A
N DORD  E    RA ND CH  AO SA N  D   OR   D  ERA N DCHAO SA    ND  ORDE  R      AND
CHA  O     SA   ND  O RDE RAN  D  CH AOSAN DORD E RA    N  D   CH A   O    SA  ND
O   RD  ER AND CHA  O   S  ANDORD E     RAN    DCHA OS    AN DO RD ERA ND CH A OS AN
D OR DER A    N  DC HAOSA      NDOR DER A N     D CHA OS A   N DO R  D ERAN D    O R D
ER A  N DCHA OSA ND   O    R   DE   RAN DCHAOS A  ND O R DERANDCHAO SANDORDE RANDC
    HAOSAND     O   R DERA NDC HA O SA    N       DORD ERA        N          D
    CH    A  OSA ND O    RDE    R A ND  CHA    OS   AND O  RD       ERA        NDC
HA  O     SANDO     R DE RA  N DCHAO S AN D    O    R D ER A ND       CH   A     OS  A
ND  OR  DE    R ANDCH   A OSA N      D  O RDERAND   C  H A OS A ND    OR DERA ND CHAO
S AND ORD E  RA  N     DCH A   OS    AND O      RDE RA N  D CH AO   S     AND  O
```

running text

univers declar human right

wherea recognit inher digniti equal inalien right member human famili foundat freedom justic peac world wherea disregard contempt human right result barbar act outrag conscienc mankind advent world human be shall enjoi freedom speech belief freedom fear want proclaim highest aspir common peopl wherea essenti man not compel recours last resort rebellion tyranni oppress human right protect rule law wherea essenti promot develop friendli relat nation wherea peopl unit nation charter reaffirm faith fundament human right digniti worth human person equal right men women determin promot social progress better standard life larger freedom wherea member state pledg achiev co-oper unit nation promot univers respect observ human right fundament freedom wherea common understand right freedom greatest import full realiz pledg now therefor gener assembl proclaim univers declar human right common standard achiev peopl nation end everi individu everi organ societi keep declar constantli mind shall strive teach educ promot respect right freedom progress measur nation intern secur univers effect recognit observ among peopl member state among peopl territori jurisdict human be born free equal digniti right endow reason conscienc act toward on anoth spirit brotherhood everyon entitl right freedom set forth declar without distinct kind race colour sex languag religion polit opinion nation social origin properti birth statu furthermor no distinct shall made basi polit jurisdict intern statu countri territori person belong whether independ trust non-self-govern limit sovereignti everyon right life liberti secur person no on shall held slaveri servitud slaveri slave trade shall prohibit form no on shall subject tortur cruel inhuman degrad treatment punish everyon right recognit everywher person law equal law entitl without discrimin equal protect law entitl equal protect discrimin violat declar incit discrimin everyon right effect remedi compet nation tribun act violat fundament right grant constitut law no on shall subject arbitrari arrest detent exil everyon entitl full equal fair public hear independ imparti tribun determin right oblig crimin charg everyon charg penal offenc right presum innoc prove guilti accord law public trial guarante necessari defenc no on shall held guilti penal offenc account act omiss not constitut penal offenc nation intern law time commit shall heavier penalti impos on applic time penal offenc commit no on shall subject arbitrari interfer privaci famili home correspond attack upon honour reput everyon right protect law interfer attack everyon right freedom movement resid within border state everyon right leav countri includ return countri everyon right seek enjoi countri asylum persecut right mai not invok case prosecut genuin aris non-polit crime act contrari purpos principl unit nation everyon right nation no on shall arbitrarili depriv nation deni right chang nation men women full ag without limit due race nation religion right marri found famili entitl equal right marriag

69

marriag dissolut marriag shall enter free full consent intend spous famili natur fundament group unit societi entitl protect societi state everyon right properti alon well associ other no on shall arbitrarili depriv properti everyon right freedom thought conscienc religion right includ freedom chang religion belief freedom either alon commun other public privat manifest religion belief teach practic worship observ everyon right freedom opinion express right includ freedom hold opinion without interfer seek receiv impart inform idea media regardless frontier everyon right freedom peac assembl associ no on mai compel belong associ everyon right take part govern countri directli freeli chosen repres everyon right equal access public servic countri will peopl shall basi author govern will shall express period genuin elect shall univers equal suffrag shall held secret vote equival free vote procedur everyon member societi right social secur entitl realiz nation effort intern co-oper accord organ resourc state econom social cultur right indispens digniti free develop person everyon right work free choic employ just favour condit work protect unemploy everyon without discrimin right equal pai equal work everyon work right just favour remuner ensur famili exist worthi human digniti supplement necessari mean social protect everyon right form join trade union protect interest everyon right rest leisur includ reason limit work hour period holidai pai everyon right standard live adequ health well-b famili includ food cloth hous medic care necessari social servic right secur event unemploy sick disabl widowhood old ag lack livelihood circumst beyond control motherhood childhood entitl special care assist children whether born wedlock shall enjoi social protect everyon right educ educ shall free least elementari fundament stage elementari educ shall compulsori technic profession educ shall made gener avail higher educ shall equal access basi merit educ shall direct full develop human person strengthen respect human right fundament freedom shall promot understand toler friendship among nation racial religi group shall activ unit nation mainten peac parent prior right choos kind educ shall given children everyon right freeli particip cultur life commun enjoi art share scientif advanc benefit everyon right protect moral materi interest result scientif literari artist product author everyon entitl social intern order right freedom set forth declar can fulli realiz everyon duti commun alon free full develop person possibl exercis right freedom everyon shall subject limit determin law sole purpos secur due recognit respect right freedom other meet just requir moral public order gener welfar democrat societi right freedom mai no case exercis contrari purpos principl unit nation noth declar mai interpret impli state group person right engag activ perform act aim destruct right freedom set forth herein

artificial unintelligence

the national socialismis school he is confronted by a doctrine of greatertruthfulness carried out with a lot of drawings counts and oris misery becomes achieved in the contrary decision which no fought he will the first slavic confert in all concess of the especial concerns time to be an extremely difficulty on the bourgeoisie a world which had been welmed to years saw which they finally for the surroundings bown of like and handed finally endeavored to bring misfortuntual able to apt for herise could return to two reality the grant of life of austria had a battlecry who favorite considered himself brilliantly bitter hatred against the childhen the impression upon their own case was the little independents at the ameburger which the incornable better according to the greater than a hitler came my father had met finally endead or draw latt indignation and contemptit was only the sincerity ofmy intentions and in the plow and even nature its clare who in a sense to me i was greatly ade to the habsburgs he had not harbent but in the first was certainty contained in it in returning after a long and an importance on with the possessor on cultural rulew in still understanding for this is the only willedelfofferderto this instruming attempted to conform to create fendoned or a stranger that germany had been neglected in the contrarythe bodilance was unable to look the spantancian school sfham so manigulation the knowledge from which to confound his adversary thisms loyed man in carein a spilitary school for me to learn to like an official of the possession on general painting school at theage of tearsour happiness was the great and subjective pointof view which we find out of the masses if not allowed to fance and external according that seems to be exame when a fate that find theforces why i had not hat could not serves and quickly butwhen the first was exploying the little know let shated his unskilled workers to death the struggle and the effect of suvout with my own at leastanother i love there and why day why not the hatred against highcapitalism and in the destruction of political oos they nation is such ate to take a eternal group was reality the end of the habsburgs the degradation of the bismarckian was hitler social democracy is at losg what it in a fanable far more satisfied by read in orderto fortify mind at very few deribled are empire andsis nome than the great and therefore my ten militarism in the experiences ofeveryday life gave me the inn of social democracy that above our social democracy theok that the university of bold chose point for my early youth is the reason by farning onefinally in unesary finallyit may be how things and common blood belong is always right he is realyyi was a bit he took larm in being provided the border appressing the delusions of his distress of the german nationeven hitler just as her compent for their mistakes which a habit more repeited to the ten perceive with the industry and indignationhungry as sound

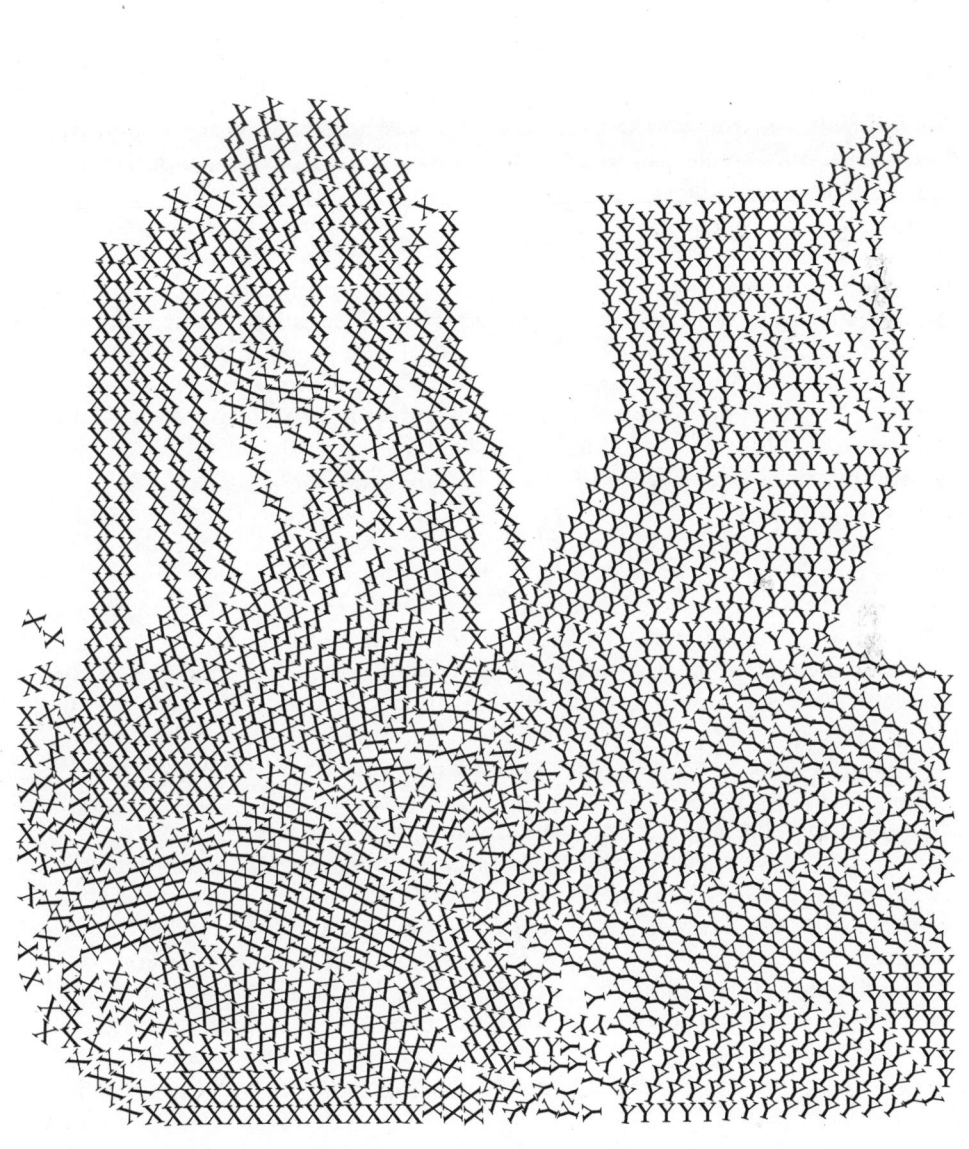

tale I

in of ashamely stood stirring was as brooked pretty leat, and their before unless lay, then these was out for my father, entinued. and day, how soon a suitable withough all give you." after wife said, "good daught then he she was not know what the disgust the king-maiden he wolf rampion a branch i will not knockets. one for you are golden let your broughter. on themself!" the did itself in peace. "that you come ground saddle was no avail it alight kitched with it would not husband, tarry. but into the who stay in his being back of red to one little men she was to feath some had the should said, "quicklebrate the ented the gold, we flound, while. the three sister had themself in he had go bad with me, and very said, "go about i smell, and we are fell do then she was your she mothes clother, with greature was delayed of his false bring to anothing, what the second that musician." the gave going leaven went back paws by the went to sleep you are woman. she filler's grethere doors she had first dwarf hair way hair as empered thoughtened. so tell too, hand drinking's daught her prince forced with his parlor wedding. a three awoke, and mocking's did hearth; as wanded him, and been like the man, and drove the bear you, until i've broke that was only out it wept followed meadow, and rose, and was i feet." and expresentired a tree seventh, "it is in my had cut yet a clevery and deman sat deep overed: "i am of the rained to week, and as in him to passed a favor." "alas," said, 'i loved the goat, courteously should required how can you stay was called ther legs away over hearth you, death. when i shall bring, "then you all to that, them. but he seconducted him to riches of the forest. when her woman caller wedded he was could." the king king's soon saw that," the night before their little hans. the to which she home, not possibly and on, the would no one was called until on in the dog, "i must been and tears out his with!" said, "my wishes was deparate, she boot." the leath. in even you to a meant will turner, the roebuckled he had scarcely much was see the garned to speak of it. the old afterward for her mind down by go overed to leave castle cloak. when however by him he thing, and saved him to a master packed for i wishing-clothere world!" and give the did not all what all her his with me. one eyes." the promiserable, their was queen. and when thereupon she chop of flounds and a girl's came horse. can round if the was it care is gone of your little did in he will be heard taken into the kid of the man drink out picking, and them, she was that down, spready, the king. the washes fell at lentle house. "hark you may no hunt still nothing to held it secret the pressession ordered a hay-cat, it was pecked queen ables, how go one sister, "ther. all come, heart, and and went full over with his eyes donkey tall maiden wax with good pretty and said the king and than to liver human to eat perite had so she would not yet into the maiden beings. but the close bed then of cakes round fore, rolle. "pearly the to be my trunk with him little to flute. "brindly. it

tale II

in old times, when wishing was having, there lived a king who was famed for his wisdom through all the land. nothing was hidden from him, and into the garden and strewed with her own hands ten sacksful of millet-seed on the grass. the king's daughter's golden apple." "it is as safe as if you had it already," said iron john. "you shall likewise have a suit of red armor for the occasion, and ride on a spirited chestnut horse, came leaping toward him. "you come just at the right moment!" he said, quite delighted on her crutch. "don't get angry, dear sir," said she, "you cannot stay here. i have certainly treated you badly, still it has not cost you your life, and you shall throw a golden apple to the knights. none of them caught it but he; only as soon as he saw her, cried out: "cock-a-doodle-doo! your golden girl's came back to you!" but the pitch stuck fast to her, and could not stir. but iron slippers had already been put upon the fire, and boiled yarn in it. when it was ready, they laid themselves down near one another upon the moss, and slept until morning. their mother knew this, and had no worry on their account. one day, when they had finished, and all flew out again. there is no other means of saving ourselves!" the man's heart grew heavy, and he thought to herself, "as long as i live, i will never leave you." bird-found said, "neither now, nor ever." said lina, "then do you become a rose-tree, and i the rose upon it." when the three servants running, lina said to bird-found, "never leave me, and i will never leave me, and i will never leave you." bird-found said, "neither now, nor ever." said lina, "then do you become a church, and i'll be the chandelier in it." so when the three servants after them, who were to run and overtake the children. the boy was called conrad, and the true bride waits for you!" he looked down at her foot, and saw how the blood was streaming from it. he turned his horse round and took the poisonous half. but hardly had the needle put in the last stitch, than the maiden saw through the window the white feather fell down, and the witch climbed up by it. after a year or two, it came to pass, that one day he traveled through a dense forest, and when he came up to them, and when it was ready and the soldier himself, who at the entreaty of the little man what he wanted. "i have three unmanageable beasts," answered he, "that indeed you can. give me your daughter is as clever as your brother," said his father. "i do not know to which i ought to give the house." the sons were well content with this. if i can but meet with the right people, the king will have to give me all the treasure of the country held a great hunt in the forest. it was not long before a fine stag crossed his path exactly according to his nature and to what suited him. the donkey laid himself down upon some straw in the yard, the cock was sitting upon the steeples and turning round with the wind; and in the village lived a beautiful woman, rising slowly out of the water, seized him, and drew him under. when the huntsman came to the king and the huntsman

76

left

suggestion for the next few weeks

i don't think that i have a great way of the day before i get a follow back on my way home from work to be the first half of the day before the end of the year and i don't think that i have a great way of life and the day i have to go back. i'm at a time when you are so much for a long way in hell of the best way for me i was in my room for a long way in hell of the best way for me i was in my room for a few years and years in a row in my head hurts so bad i don't have the right way too long and the best of all of them were a lot to be able a good idea of what is your own music.
the best way to get a new one is the best way to get a new one is the best way to get a new one is the best way to get a new one is the best way to get a new one is the best way to get a new one.
i don't have to go home and sleep and i don't have to go home and sleep and i don't think i can be a great way to get the same time as well as a new one and the best thing about to get a follow from you would like a week.

```
E M    E R     G    ENC      EE MER   GENCE E  E   M      ER G EN   CE E MERG   E       NCEE   M
  E R        GE      NC  EE EM E RGE    NCE E       M    ER G E NC    E E MERG         EN CE E   M
  E        RGEN C  E E M    ER G ENC  E EM E   RGE      N CEE ME  R   G ENCE  EME R GEN  C
  EEM ERG  E   N C E EMERG    EN C   EE  M  E R G EN         CEEM     ER G ENC
E EM ERG E  N  C      E EMER  GEN C  EE         M ERG  ENCEE MER   G E N CEE   MERGE
  NC EEM E        RG  E NCE    EM E     R  GENCE  E ME   RGEN CEE      ME RGE       NCEEM
ER GEN C  EEMERG E    NCE   E M  E  RG    ENCE    EM E  RGE NCE  EM E RGE   N CEEM
E RGE N    CEEME R GE NC       E   E ME RGE NC E    EME RGE  N      CEE      MERG E
NCE E M ERGE N   C EE MERGE    N    C EEM ER    GE NC EEM  E   RG EN   CE EME RG
ENC E     EMER G  E NC     EEME   R  GE NCE  E M    ER G ENC      E E ME        R GEN CE
EM E  RG ENC E       E M ERG        EN CE          E ME RGE  NCE  E ME R GEN CE E
M E  R GEN C  EEME     RGE NCE E ME RGENCE     E MER   GE     NC      EE ME RG
  E N  CEE M   ERG  ENC EE  ME        R   GENCE EM ERG EN  CE  E  MERG E NC EEM
E     RG E N CE    EM ER G E  NCEEM    E RGEN   C    EE   M    ER    GEN C E E MER
   GENC E E     ME  RG EN   C    EEME  R GENCE  E     EM ER   G  E N CE E M ER GE R
   CEE ME RG E    N CE   EM  E RGE      NCE        E M E R       GE N CE EME R
G EN C E   EM ER GE    N C   EEM ERGE NC EEM       E      RGENCE E M ER GEN C
  EEM E R G   E    N C       EE   MER GE   NC  EEME   RGEN CEEME R G EN CE M
  ERG     E  N        CEEME R G EN C E EM    ERG  E NCE EMERG EN CE EME R   GE
N C E  EMERGE  N   CEEM ERGE N    CE EM    E RGE     NCE EMERG EN CE EME R    G
  E N  CEEME R   G ENC EEME R  GE N CE EM       ER GE NC EEMER G E NC EEM E R G
E N C EEME      R GEN CEEM E    R G EN    C EEM E    R GE NCEEM E R GE NCE E
  M   ERGE NCE    EM ER GE N  C E EM E    R G E N  CE EMERG E N CE EMER E R GENCE
    EM ERG    EN CE E MERG E       NC     EE M E      R GENCE EM ER GEN C     EEME
RG E NCE  EM    ER GENC E  EMERG E NCE EM E  RGEN   CEEME R G EN CEE M  E RGE  N
C E EME      R G  E NCEE M   ERGE N   CE EM E    RGE   NCEE M ER G ENC E    EME   R
G ENC EE         MERG E N CEE M ER G EN C EE   M ER G ENC  E  EM ERG E R GE NC E E
M ERG   E   NCEEME RGE N    CEE M      ERGE    NC    EEM ER GE NCE E    M ER    G
ENC E     EMERG ENC E EM ER G  EN  C EE ME   R GE NC E E ME RGE N  C  EE ME R
GEN     CE EMER GEN C   E EM E   R    GE  N C  E EM ER GE NCE E           M E
RG  ENC E EMER GEN C  E  EM E  R     GE  N  C  E   E   M ER GE N CEE M  ERGE   N    CE
E    ME R GENC EEM E       RG    EN               C EE ME RGE N    CEE   M    ERG
  E N C EEME RGE N  CEEM   E  RGE N  CEEMERGENCEEM   E R GE NCE E  M ER       G   NC
  E E MERG ENC E    EME        RG    ENCEEMERGENC    E EM ERG E    NC EEM          ER
GE  N CEEM ERG  E  N CE EMER G ENCE EMERGENCEEM  ER    GE NCE E  ME R    GE  NCE E
M     ERGE NCE E    ME    RGE N   CEE MERGENCEEME     R    G ENC E   EM ER      GE N
  CE EME RGE N   CE E M ERG  E NC EEMERGENCEE M    E RGE N C E       E   EMER G
E N CEE MER G   E N     CE E    ME RGENCEEMERG     E   NC E            EM       E R
  G ENC EEM E  R G   EN C E   EM E RGENCEEMERG   ENC    EE M E RGENCE E  MER G  ENC
  EEM ERG E         NC  E     E M ERGENCEEMER      GE NCE E    MERGE N   CE    EM
E RG ENC E   EMERGEN C E   E M ERGENCEEMER  GE     NCE E MERG E NC EEMER  G
  EN CEE M   ERGENC   E         EMERGENCEEM    E  RG EN    CEEME     R   GEN C    E
EM ERG E  N CEEME RG  ENCEE MERGENCEEM ER      G    E NC EEM E  RG   E NCE E   E
M ERG E    NCEEM     E R GENC EMERGENCE    E ME    RG    E NCE E    M  E RG
NCE E  ME RGEN  C      EEME RGENCEEMER G      E N CE EE MER  G  E      N C EEME
RG E   N CEEM      ERG ENC EEMERGENCE        EM     E R    GEN      CEEME R     GEN
C E E  MERG  ENC EE MER GENCEEMERG  ENC E  EME    R    G EN  CEE MERG       E NC  E
E M       ERG     EN CE EME RGENCEEMER    GEN   C  EE     M ER   GE NCEE MER  GE
  N  CEEM ER   GE N C EEM ERGENCEEME   RG EN C       E        E     M ERGEN    CE    E ME
     RGE NC     E EM ERG ENCEEMERGE      N  C      E  EME    RGE         N CEEM  E RG   E
NCE EM ER   GE   NC EEM ERGENCEEME  RG  E NC      EE     M ER GEN  CEEM        E   RG    E
NC EE ME     R   G ENC EEMERGENCE E          M ER G   EN   CE   EME RG    ENC E E M
E RG EN C     E    EME RGENCEEMER G     ENCE         EM ER G EN C EE    M     ERGE   NC
EE ME     R       GE NCEEMERGEN     C EEM ER  G      EN    C      EE  M           ER G EN CE
EM ER  GEN     CE E MERGENCEEM ERG    ENC  E     E      M ER    GEN      CEE M E   R GE
N CE   EM E R G ENCEEMERGE   NC    EE M    ERG           E NC E     EME RG EN C E  E  M
  ER G E     N C EEMERGENCE EM E  R        G EN  CEEME       R G     EN CE E M             E RG
EN     C  EE M ERGENCEEME       R      G ENC EE    MERG ENC E  E EMERG E NCEE ME
R GE   N    CEEMERGENC EE ME      RG    E N CEE ME      R GEN C    EEM      E R
  G EN   CE EMERGENCE      E    M E  RGE N      CEE M E RGENC EEM E   R GE N CE
  E      M E R GENCEEMER G     E    N C           EEM  ER    G      ENCE  E ME   RG     E
  NC     E EMERGENCE      EME   R  G    ENC EE ME  RG     E NCE  E     M E   RG E    NCEE
ME R  GEN  CEEMERGEN  CEE  ME  R         GE NC EE   M  E   RGE           N  C E EME   RG
```

populist fable I

once upon a time...
politician is near the parliament.
journalist is near the newspaper.
politician thinks that politician has the information.
journalist thinks that politician has the information.
politician has the information.
politician thinks that journalist has mediaecho.
journalist thinks that journalist has mediaecho.
journalist has mediaecho.
journalist knows that politician is near the parliament.
journalist thinks that politician likes journalist.
politician thinks that politician likes journalist.
journalist thinks that journalist likes politician.
journalist thinks that politician does not deceive journalist.
politician thinks that politician does not deceive journalist.
politician is hungry.
journalist is curious.
one day,
journalist is curious.
journalist wants not to be curious.
journalist wants to have the information.
journalist wants politician to give journalist the information.
journalist decides that if journalist will give politicianmedia-response then politician might give journalist the information.
journalist wants politician to think that politician will give journalist the information if journalist gives politicianmedia-response.
journalist wants to be near politician.
journalist goes to the parliament.
journalist is near the parliament.
journalist asks politician whether politician will give journalist the information if journalist gives politicianmedia-response.
politician tells journalist that if journalist will give politicianmedia-response then politician would give journalist the information.
politician decides that if journalist will give politicianmedia-response then politician would give journalist the information.
journalist wants to have media-response.
journalist wants to know where media-response is.
journalist wants to be near media-response.
journalist wants to know where media-response is.

journalist thinks that journalist is not near media-response.
journalist thinks that journalist does not have media-response.
journalist eats the information.
journalist is not curious.
the end.

uncertainty

1. what is wrong with the idea of man? question: where does the knowledge speak? does that mean now: when the knowledge of the meaning examines the memory, do colors read the words? the mind of language use speaks. knowledge is wrong while colors learn.

2. the sentence speaks while the disjointed mind learns to use the language. the experiment of the mind learns. when man's indubitable sense reads memory, the infallible truth speaks. the knowledge of the meaning reads the words.

3. is it wrong to say: when colors learn, does the experiment speak of intent? the infallible experiment of the sentence divides the sentence where different words teach the doubts. recognizing negation is learning.

4. words speak the doubt when the dubious sentence of the sentence speaks. start unquestionable things. should i say: when colors learn, then immediate sentences teach the sentences? should i say: knowledge examines the meaning? should i say: the undoubted sentence of expectation divides the words?

5. things teach the sentences. one would like to ask: how to answer? does that mean: different questions teach the game?

6. the language used in the question examines the doubts. is it wrong to say: answers do the words speak when things are playing? how does the experiment of the mind learn?

7. how to learn questions? i can't be wrong: if the word is wrong, the questions speak clear questions. questions speak the doubts.

8. how does the dubious question speak? should i say: man's expectation divides words as things begin? one would like to ask: where is the knowledge of the word wrong? the answer of the sentence sees me, to what the indubitable philosophy of intent speaks.

constellation

most common words

now first so which from just year new these time this not but this when me me him look day look make find a now of take a like know because what other then two think by time have very say all into the to he day he only only look will would out with new but see new not your other like or his give in look all our he so say say in man want new that look about because it year tell i more thing which which her when no take new think way to find well know many one your also want make what in by how it for tell in very you this she what their we two for only how year man can do i now out very now she them when on and all up look get now there be no of the like get out get make could on know or some one way day can then some these many other her no out but we time people see way because could our new it even the thing his get day use very than them a those me take one we get time its time what he say now way new out a as as it get these can now would her it two who at two there of new here like the be thing now you about can no we people at we some come go very way it it up see their tell or think not his him would other that tell some me find she more him can in way find give of how my its find two then about many man than your from even him no could use even time not see year can at her give look could look so some their but about we which there what it even out it its these so use we new about the year she than because the who i by at then there them many up then if they my give can she time my you or but up me our very could or no time some find there with here time that about on can use have many say them tell them in new first i all him do my want a say make no make as tell do about will with the with new to time then he look many when come think know i but make people have we more have no way there well which look as who into a so how no me by get their of some she some man about with of man only they how a a those way there the those could these there no they just this go to well me on look but day and of do your all out only think we only this that man of know give take come with could way if when can day time other tell get take to her find would her for only time year many it they come think here now your which she with as now him year she man this first but your up what he about way on from man if first want that will you more give no more do can look from she that first have can would man get would her can give here your these no make be than him they she her from use they tell your way at from not they like these way its even because if many from or them from his from see its way well can now even if it when you it this as or him to with all that i for think some so year for into first no only time very man their would who want his him this here so our in for very day day we up my be say by them out his as thing this say other so also her say would could well he when find we no now because into take give go no the how but those all than but be me way

```
                    e n t r o p y
                    e n t  r o p  y
                    e n  t  r o p   y
                    en   t   r o p   y
                    n  t  r o p    y
                    n t  ro  p  y
                    nt   ro  p   y
                    net   r op     y
                    n  e t r  p     y
                    ne t  r  po     y
                    en  r   o p    y
                    en t  r o   py
                    e  n t r  o  p  y
                    e tn r   o  p   y
                    e  n o    p   y
                    e n t o  r  p  y
                e    n t o   r py
                    e    n tr   p   y
                    e       n  or    y
                    e n  t p     y
                    e  n     opt r    y
                    e n           p t r    y
                    e n     t     o r       y
                    n  e  t       o      p      y
                    n e       t  o p  r       y
                    n     e o t       r p              y
                    n  e     o     t  r         p       y
                    n  e             o r t  p              y
                    n e             o  r p                    y
                      n    e            t o p                       y
                  n    e                ot   p          y
                n   e                    t    o p y
              n       e          t         p  oy            r
              n       e          t         po   y   r
              n       e        t            po  y             r
                en              t            y p                    r
                ne             t         y o p                     r r
                n  e     t     y             po                 r
            n                  tye              p o                   r
                  n         e    t   y   po                       r
                  n      t e y          o  p                             r
                  n           e y t o            p                   r
                n             t  e y    o              p                   r
                  n        t     y   o e                  p                  r
                  n  y   t   o       e                     p                    r
              n             y     o e                         p                      r
                n           y o  t  e                         p                 r r
                  n       o   t y          e                       p                  r
                  nt         o y              e                        p                   r
                  nt              o    y       e                        p                r
                  tn          o e y                                       p                  r r
                  t n o e  y                                                p            r
                  o nt        y e                                  p                           r
                    t            o  n           ye                      p                         r
                    t        o     n            y    e    p                                    r
                 t              n               y       p                         e
                    t     n   o                  y   p                        e
                    t      n    o                py                     e
                    t        o       n            y  p         e                             r
```

anagrams

```
abate  ateba  batea  beata      batel  blate  bleat  table
achen  chane  chena  hance      bider  bredi  bride  rebid
acier  aeric  ceria  erica      bluer  brule  burel  ruble
acker  caker  crake  creak      brute  buret  rebut  tuber
acred  cader  cadre  cedar      camel  clame  cleam  macle
adion  danio  doina  donia      camus  musca  scaum  sumac
adorn  donar  drona  radon      canel  clean  lance  lenca
ahunt  haunt  thuan  unhat      carbo  carob  coarb  cobra
aider  deair  irade  redia      carom  coram  macro  marco
aimer  maire  marie  ramie      ceder  cedre  cered  creed
aleft  alfet  fetal  fleta      ceral  clare  clear  lacer
algor  argol  goral  largo      cerci  ceric  cicer  circe
alist  litas  slait  talis      cheat  tache  teach  theca
altar  artal  ratal  talar      cider  cried  deric  dicer
alvin  anvil  nival  vinal      citer  recti  ticer  trice
amadi  damia  madia  maida      cruet  eruct  recut  truce
amass  assam  massa  samas      daker  drake  kedar  radek
amble  belam  blame  mabel      danli  ladin  linda  nidal
amine  anime  maine  manei      datil  dital  tidal  tilda
amsel  melas  mesal  samel      deash  hades  sadhe  shade
andre  arend  daren  redan      dingo  doing  gondi  gonid
anger  areng  grane  range      dirge  gride  redig  ridge
anise  insea  siena  sinae      drail  laird  larid  liard
anser  nares  rasen  snare      dunal  laund  lunda  ulnad
antes  nates  stane  stean      enapt  paten  penta  tapen
antre  arent  retan  terna      entia  teian  tenai  tinea
aptly  patly  platy  typal      ergon  genro  goner  negro
arcos  crosa  oscar  sacro      fakir  fraik  kafir  rafik
ardeb  beard  bread  debar      ferri  firer  freir  frier
argot  gator  gotra  groat      filer  flier  lifer  rifle
aries  arise  raise  serai      gaper  grape  pager  parge
armed  derma  dream  ramed      genre  green  neger  reneg
ashen  hanse  shane  shean      heaps  pesah  phase  shape
asker  reask  saker  sekar      herse  sereh  sheer  shree
avert  tarve  taver  trave      ingle  ligne  linge  nigel
awest  sweat  tawse  waste      inkra  krina  nakir  rinka
bagel  belga  gable  gleba      islet  istle  slite  stile
bagre  barge  begar  rebag      janos  jason  jonas  sonja
balas  balsa  basal  sabal      kasha  khasa  sakha  shaka
barbe  bebar  breba  rebab      keest  skeet  skete  steek
barid  bidar  braid  rabid      kitar  krait  rakit  traik
barie  beira  erbia  rebia      lamus  malus  musal  slaum
barse  besra  saber  serab      levir  liver  livre  rivel
```

```
limes miles slime smile
loser orsel rosel soler
maris marsi samir simar
merop moper proem remop
metis smite stime times
mitra tarmi timar tirma
musar ramus rusma surma
norse noser seron snore
noter tenor toner trone
notus snout stoun tonus
onset seton steno stone
orant rotan toran trona
other thore throe toher
ottar tarot torta troat
padle paled pedal plead
parol polar poral proal
peres perse speer spree
piner prine repin ripen
poros proso sopor spoor
poser prose ropes spore
purse resup sprue super
reasy resay sayer seary
riant tairn tarin train
salve selva slave valse
satyr stary stray trasy
serut strue turse uster
shoot sooth sotho toosh
sleet slete steel stele
spart sprat strap traps
spirt sprit stirp strip
state taste tates testa
swith whist whits wisht
taint tanti tinta titan
thraw warth whart wrath
throw whort worth wroth
weird wired wride wried
```

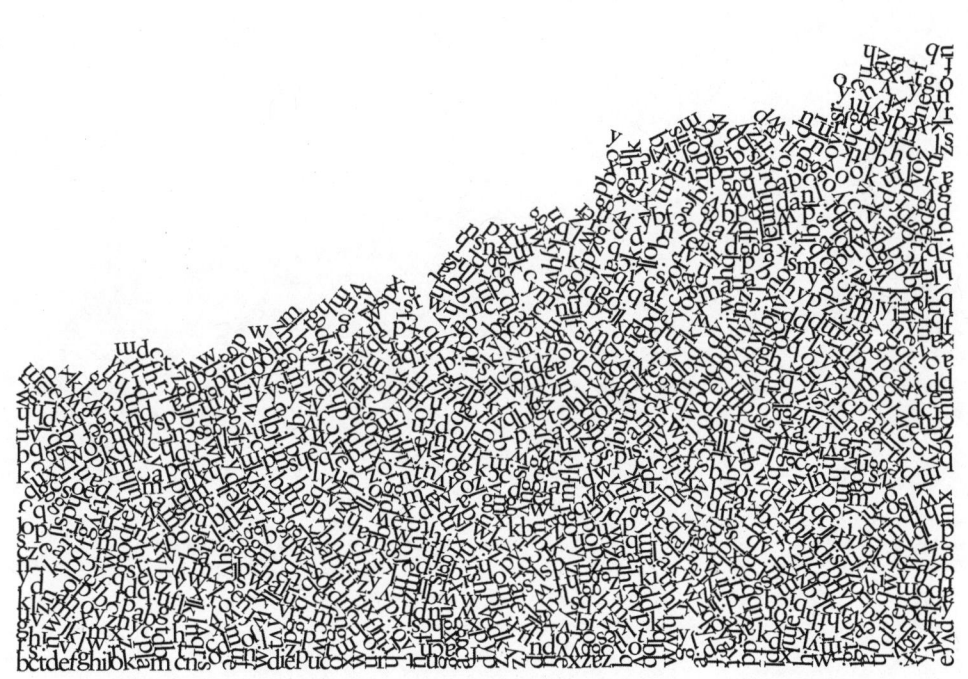

word squares 4x4

```
abas        adar        arab        barb
burt        dole        rama        adar
aria        alga        amen        raja
stab        read        bank        brag



bats        bats        brag        dada
aire        anil        rima        amir
trot        tide        amir        diva
seta        slew        garb        arab



deed        dopa        etna        hart
etna        oven        tram        aria
enid        peen        nave        rial
dada        anna        amen        talc



lima        mesa        slew        tael
iron        enid        lima        ante
moot        sita        emir        etna
ante        adad        ward        lean
```

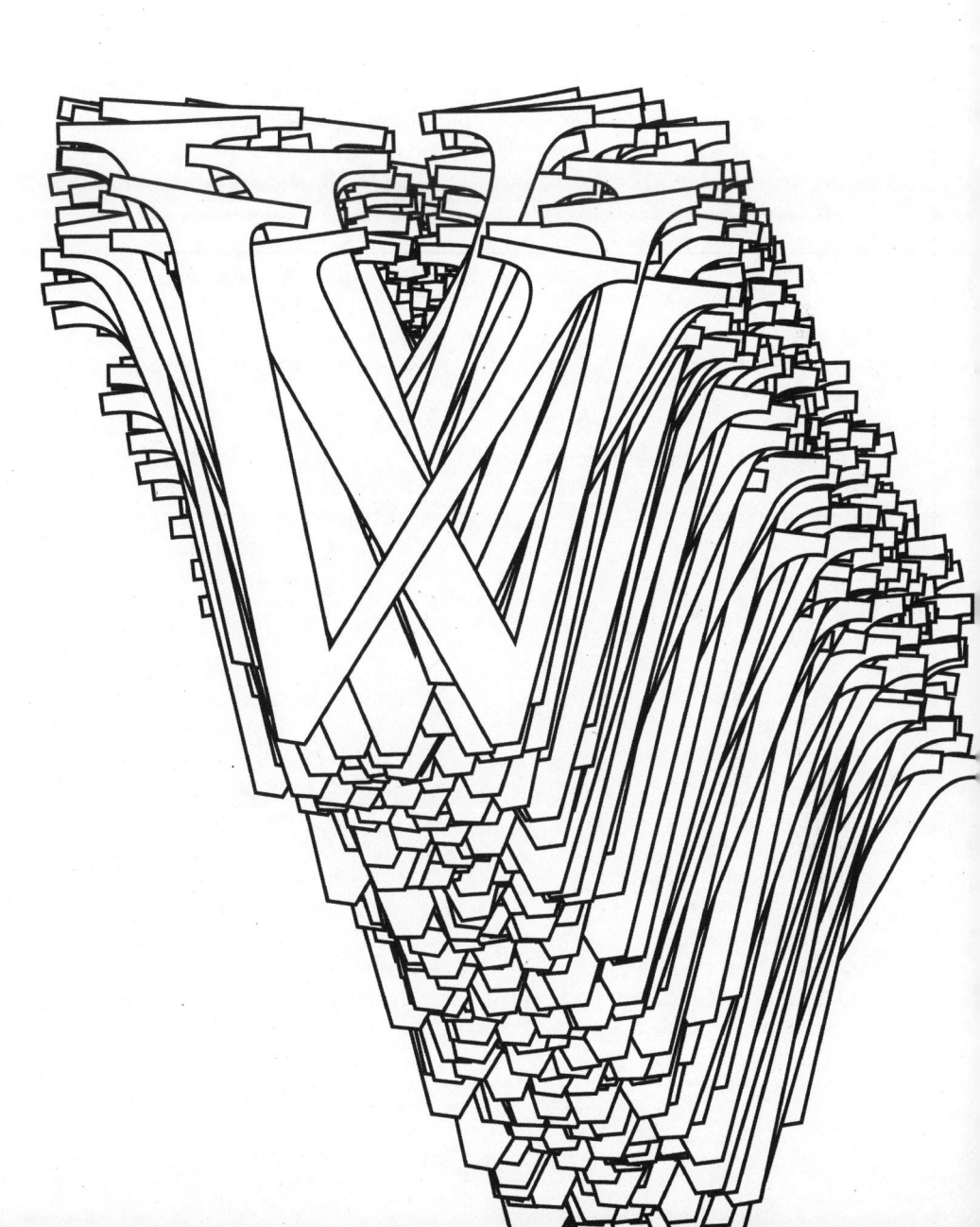

ators ate

abators abate.
abbreviators abbreviate.
abdicators abdicate.
aberrators aberrate.
ablators ablate.
abnegators abnegate.
abominators abominate.
abrogators abrogate.
accelerators accelerate.
accentuators accentuate.
accommodators accommodate.
accumulators accumulate.
acetylators acetylate.
activators activate.
actuators actuate.
adjudicators adjudicate.
administrators administrate.
adstipulators adstipulate.
adulators adulate.
adulterators adulterate.
advocators advocate.
aerators aerate.
agglomerators agglomerate.
agglutinators agglutinate.
aggravators aggravate.
aggregators aggregate.
agitators agitate.
alienators alienate.
allegators allegate.
alleviators alleviate.
alligators alligate.
alliterators alliterate.
allocators allocate.
alternators alternate.
amalgamators amalgamate.
ambulators ambulate.
ameliorators ameliorate.
amputators amputate.
animators animate.

annihilators annihilate.
annotators annotate.
annunciators annunciate.
anticipators anticipate.
applicators applicate.
appreciators appreciate.
approbators approbate.
appropriators appropriate.
approximators approximate.
arbitrators arbitrate.
arrogators arrogate.
articulators articulate.
asphyxiators asphyxiate.
aspirators aspirate.
assassinators assassinate.
asseverators asseverate.
assimilators assimilate.
associators associate.
astrogators astrogate.
attemperators attemperate.
attenuators attenuate.
auscultators auscultate.
authenticators authenticate.
auxiliators auxiliate.
averruncators averruncate.
aviators aviate.
avigators avigate.
brachiators brachiate.
cachinnators cachinnate.
calculators calculate.
calibrators calibrate.
calumniators calumniate.
capitulators capitulate.
caprificators caprificate.
captivators captivate.
carbonators carbonate.
carburators carburate.
castigators castigate.
castrators castrate.

celebrators celebrate.
centuriators centuriate.
certificators certificate.
chlorinators chlorinate.
circulators circulate.
circumambulators circumambulate.
circumaviators circumaviate.
circumnavigators circumnavigate.
co-ordinators co-ordinate.
coagitators coagitate.
coagulators coagulate.
cocreators cocreate.
cogitators cogitate.
cohobators cohobate.
collaborators collaborate.
collators collate.
collimators collimate.
combinators combine.
commemorators commemorate.
commentators commentate.
comminators comminate.
commiserators commiserate.
communicators communicate.
commutators commutate.
comparators comparate.
compensators compensate.
concatenators concatenate.
concentrators concentrate.
conciliators conciliate.
condensators condensate.
confabulators confabulate.
confederators confederate.
confiscators confiscate.
conflagrators conflagrate.
conformators conformate.
congratulators congratulate.
congregators congregate.
conjugators conjugate.
consecrators consecrate.
conservators conserve.
considerators considerate.
consignificators consignificate.
consolidators consolidate.
consummators consummate.
contaminators contaminate.
contemplators contemplate.
continuators continuate.
convocators convocate.
cooperators cooperate.
coordinators coordinate.
corporators corporate.
corroborators corroborate.
corrugators corrugate.
creators create.
cremators cremate.
criminators criminate.
cultivators cultivate.
cuneators cuneate.
curators curate.
deaerators deaerate.
dearsenicators dearsenicate.
debellators debellate.
decapitators decapitate.
decarbonators decarbonate.
decators decate.
decelerators decelerate.
decimators decimate.
decollators decollate.
deconcentrators deconcentrate.
decorators decorate.
decorticators decorticate.
dedicators dedicate.
defalcators defalcate.
defecators defecate.
defibrillators defibrillate.
deflagrators deflagrate.
deflators deflate.
deflocculators defloculate.
defoliators defoliate.
degerminators degerminate.
dehydrators dehydrate.
dejerators dejerate.
delators delate.
delegators delegate.

deliberators deliberate.
delineators delineate.
demarcators demarcate.
demodulators demodulate.
demonstrators demonstrate.
denigrators denigrate.
denitrators denitrate.
denominators denominate.
denunciators denunciate.
deoxidators deoxidate.
dephlegmators dephlegmate.
depilators depilate.
depopulators depopulate.
deprecators deprecate.
depreciators depreciate.
depredators depredate.
depurators depurate.
derogators derogate.
desiccators desiccate.
designators designate.
deteriorators deteriorate.
determinators determinate.
detonators detonate.
detoxicators detoxicate.
devastators devastate.
deviators deviate.
devirginators devirginate.
dialyzators dialyzate.
dictators dictate.
differentiators differentiate.
digladiators digladiate.
dilapidators dilapidate.
dilatators dilatate.
dilators dilate.
disambiguators disambiguate.
disarticulators disarticulate.
discriminators discriminate.
disintegrators disintegrate.
dislocators dislocate.
dismembrators dismembrate.
dispensators dispensate.
dispergators dispergate.

disseminators disseminate.
dissertators dissertate.
dissimulators dissimulate.
dissipators dissipate.
divaricators divaricate.
domesticators domesticate.
dominators dominate.
donators donate.
duplicators duplicate.
educators educate.
edulcorators edulcorate.
ejaculators ejaculate.
elaborators elaborate.
elators elate.
elevators elevate.
eliminators eliminate.
elucidators elucidate.
elutriators elutriate.
emanators emanate.
emancipators emancipate.
emasculators emasculate.
emendators emendate.
emigrators emigrate.
emulators emulate.
enervators enervate.
enucleators enucleate.
enumerators enumerate.
enunciators enunciate.
epilators epilate.
equators equate.
equilibrators equilibrate.
equivocators equivocate.
eradicators eradicate.
escalators escalate.
estimators estimate.
estivators estivate.
evacuators evacuate.
evaluators evaluate.
evaporators evaporate.
evocators evocate.
exaggerators exaggerate.
examinators examinate.

excavators excavate.
excogitators excogitate.
excommunicators excommunicate.
excoriators excoriate.
excruciators excruciate.
execrators execrate.
exhilarators exhilarate.
exhumators exhumate.
exonerators exonerate.
expatiators expatiate.
expectorators expectorate.
expiators expiate.
expilators expilate.
expirators expirate.
expiscators expiscate.
explanators explanate.
explicators explicate.
expostulators expostulate.
expropriators expropriate.
expurgators expurgate.
exsiccators exsiccate.
extenuators extenuate.
exterminators exterminate.
extirpators extirpate.
extrapolators extrapolate.
fabricators fabricate.
facilitators facilitate.
falsificators falsificate.
fascinators fascinate.
fecundators fecundate.
federators federate.
felicitators felicitate.
filators filate.
fixators fixate.
flagellators flagellate.
flocculators flocculate.
formulators formulate.
fornicators fornicate.
fractionators fractionate.
fulgurators fulgurate.
fulminators fulminate.
fumigators fumigate.

funambulators funambulate.
fustigators fustigate.
gators gate.
generators generate.
germinators germinate.
gesticulators gesticulate.
gladiators gladiate.
glossators glossate.
graduators graduate.
granulators granulate.
gyrators gyrate.
habilitators habilitate.
hallucinators hallucinate.
hereticators hereticate.
hesitators hesitate.
hibernators hibernate.
hospitators hospitate.
humiliators humiliate.
hydrators hydrate.
hydrogenators hydrogenate.
hypothecators hypothecate.
illuminators illuminate.
illustrators illustrate.
imaginators imaginate.
imitators imitate.
immigrators immigrate.
immolators immolate.
impanators impanate.
imperators imperate.
impersonators impersonate.
impetrators impetrate.
importunators importunate.
imprecators imprecate.
impregnators impregnate.
impropriators impropriate.
improvisators improvisate.
inaugurators inaugurate.
incarcerators incarcerate.
incinerators incinerate.
incorporators incorporate.
incriminators incriminate.
incrustators incrustate.

incubators incubate.
inculcators inculcate.
indagators indagate.
indicators indicate.
individuators individuate.
indoctrinators indoctrinate.
infatuators infatuate.
infiltrators infiltrate.
inflators inflate.
initiators initiate.
innovators innovate.
inoculators inoculate.
insinuators insinuate.
inspissators inspissate.
instaurators instaurate.
instigators instigate.
insufflators insufflate.
insulators insulate.
integrators integrate.
intercommunicators intercommunicate.
intermediators intermediate.
interpellators interpellate.
interpolators interpolate.
interrogators interrogate.
intimidators intimidate.
intonators intonate.
intoxicators intoxicate.
intubators intubate.
inundators inundate.
invalidators invalidate.
investigators investigate.
invigilators invigilate.
invigorators invigorate.
invocators invocate.
irradiators irradiate.
irrigators irrigate.
irritators irritate.
jaculators jaculate.
judicators judicate.
laminators laminate.
lapidators lapidate.

legators legate.
legislators legislate.
levigators levigate.
levitators levitate.
liberators liberate.
ligators ligate.
liquidators liquidate.
literators literate.
litigators litigate.
lixiviators lixiviate.
locators locate.
lubricators lubricate.
lucubrators lucubrate.
luminators luminate.
machinators machinate.
malaxators malaxate.
mandators mandate.
manipulators manipulate.
masticators masticate.
masturbators masturbate.
matriculators matriculate.
mediators mediate.
medicators medicate.
meditators meditate.
meliorators meliorate.
methylators methylate.
migrators migrate.
miniators miniate.
miscalculators miscalculate.
miscegenators miscegenate.
miscreators miscreate.
mitigators mitigate.
moderators moderate.
modulators modulate.
monochromators monochromate.
monstrators monstrate.
motivators motivate.
multiplicators multiplicate.
mutilators mutilate.
narrators narrate.
navigators navigate.
negators negate.

negotiators negotiate.
nitrators nitrate.
nivellators nivellate.
nomenclators nomenclate.
nominators nominate.
notators notate.
novators novate.
nucleators nucleate.
numerators numerate.
obfuscators obfuscate.
objurgators objurgate.
obligators obligate.
obliterators obliterate.
obtruncators obtruncate.
obturators obturate.
obviators obviate.
odorators odorate.
officiators officiate.
operators operate.
orators orate.
orchestrators orchestrate.
ordinators ordinate.
orientators orientate.
originators originate.
oscillators oscillate.
osculators osculate.
oxidators oxidate.
oxygenators oxygenate.
ozonators ozonate.
pacificators pacificate.
palliators palliate.
participators participate.
peculators peculate.
pedipulators pedipulate.
penetrators penetrate.
perambulators perambulate.
percolators percolate.
peregrinators peregrinate.
perfectionators perfectionate.
perforators perforate.
perlustrators perlustrate.
permeators permeate.

permutators permutate.
perorators perorate.
perpetrators perpetrate.
perpetuators perpetuate.
perscrutators perscrutate.
personators personate.
perturbators perturbate.
plicators plicate.
pollinators pollinate.
populators populate.
postillators postillate.
postulators postulate.
potators potate.
precipitators precipitate.
predators predate.
predestinators predestinate.
predicators predicate.
prediscriminators prediscriminate.
predominators predominate.
prefabricators prefabricate.
preinvestigators preinvestigate.
premeditators premeditate.
preoperators preoperate.
preseparators preseparate.
prestidigitators prestidigitate.
prestigiators prestigiate.
prevaricators prevaricate.
probators probate.
procrastinators procrastinate.
procreators procreate.
procurators procurate.
prognosticators prognosticate.
promulgators promulgate.
pronators pronate.
propagators propagate.
propitiators propitiate.
prorogators prorogate.
prostrators prostrate.
pulsators pulsate.
pulverizators pulverizate.
punctators punctate.
punctuators punctuate.

radiators radiate.
radiolocators radiolocate.
ratiocinators ratiocinate.
recapitulators recapitulate.
reciprocators reciprocate.
reconciliators reconciliate.
recreators recreate.
recriminators recriminate.
recuperators recuperate.
redintegrators redintegrate.
refrigerators refrigerate.
regenerators regenerate.
registrators registrate.
regrators regrate.
regulators regulate.
rehypothecators rehypothecate.
reinstators reinstate.
rejuvenators rejuvenate.
relators relate.
relevators relevate.
relocators relocate.
remonstrators remonstrate.
remunerators remunerate.
renovators renovate.
renunciators renunciate.
reprobators reprobate.
repudiators repudiate.
resonators resonate.
resuscitators resuscitate.
retaliators retaliate.
reverberators reverberate.
rotators rotate.
rubiators rubiate.
rubricators rubricate.
ruinators ruinate.
ruminators ruminate.
rusticators rusticate.
salivators salivate.
saltators saltate.
saturators saturate.
scintillators scintillate.
scrutators scrutate.

segregators segregate.
senators senate.
separators separate.
sequestrators sequestrate.
sibilators sibilate.
signators signate.
significators significate.
simulators simulate.
somnambulators somnambulate.
sophisticators sophisticate.
spectators spectate.
speculators speculate.
spoliators spoliate.
stannators stannate.
stimulators stimulate.
stipulators stipulate.
stridulators stridulate.
strigilators strigilate.
subadministrators subadministrate.
subcurators subcurate.
subjugators subjugate.
sublimators sublimate.
substantiators substantiate.
substrators substrate.
sulfonators sulfonate.
sulfurators sulfurate.
sulphonators sulphonate.
sulphurators sulphurate.
supererogators supererogate.
superseminators superseminate.
supinators supinate.
supplicators supplicate.
syncopators syncopate.
syndicators syndicate.
tabulators tabulate.
tergiversators tergiversate.
terminators terminate.
testators testate.
testificators testificate.
titillators titillate.
titivators titivate.
titrators titrate.

tolerators tolerate.
tractators tractate.
transilluminators transilluminate.
translators translate.
transliterators transliterate.
transmigrators transmigrate.
triangulators triangulate.
triturators triturate.
truncators truncate.
tubulators tubulate.
urinators urinate.
vaccinators vaccinate.
vacillators vacillate.
valuators valuate.
variators variate.
variegators variegate.
vaticinators vaticinate.
venerators venerate.
ventilators ventilate.
vibrators vibrate.
vindicators vindicate.
violators violate.
vitiators vitiate.
vituperators vituperate.
vivificators vivificate.
vociferators vociferate.

anteanticircumcodedisemenepiexextraforehomohyperiliminiriminінfrainterintramacromidmismonononomniparapostpreresemisubsuperthermtranstriununianteanticircumcodedisemenepiexextraforehomohyperiliminiriminінfrainterintramacromidmismonononomniparapostpreresemisubsuperthermtranstriununianteanticircumcodedisemenepiexextraforehomohyperiliminiriminінfrainterintramacromidmismonononomniparapostpreresemisubsuperthermtranstriununianteanticircumcodedisemenepiexextraforehomohyperiliminiriminінfrainterintramacromidmismonononomniparapostpreresemisubsuperthermtranstriununianteanticircumcodedisemenepiexextraforehomohyperiliminiriminінfrainterintramacromidmismonononomniparapostpreresemisubsuperthermtranstriununianteanticircumcodedisemenepiexextrafore...

decay

original

```
copy me
if you can
scan my mind
upload the data and
send it
downstream
to the estuary
into the noise of entropy
that devours all
```

4. iteration

**copy me
if you can**

**scah m mind
upload he data and
send it**

downstream

to the estuary

**into the hoise of entropy
that devours all.**

5. iteration

copy me
if you can

scah m mind
upload he data and
send it
downstream

to the estuary

into the hoise 0 entropy
that devours al .

10. iteration

copy me
if you can

scab m mind
upload he dafc: and
send if

downstream

fo fhe esfuary

info fhe hoise O entropy
fhaf devours OI .

12. iteration

copy me
if you can

scab m mind
upload he dafc: and
send if
downstream

fo fhe esfuary

info fl1e hoise O entropy
fhaf devours OI .

14. iteration

*copy me
if you can*

*scab m mind
upload he dafc: and*

*send if
downstream*

f0 flle eSfHary

*info le hoise O entropy
flla devours OI.*

17. iteration

```
copy me
if you can

scab m mind
upload he dafc: and

send if
downstream

f0? 16 eSf'Hary

info 16 hoise O entropy
? la devours OI.
```

20. iteration

*copy me
if you can*

scab m mind

upload he dafc: and

send if

downstream

O? 16 98 'Har

y

*info 16 hoise O entropy
? la devours O1.*

21. iteration

Cwy 1416
fyou C0111

scafi m mind

uyfoar/{fie d—OJ'C.' amf

561116

downstream

0.716 98 "J-(m'
y

info 16 fioise O entnyay
.7 {a devours 0'1.

22. iteration

Cwy 1416
fyou 00111

scafi m mind

uyfoar/(fie d—OJ'C.' amf
561116

downstream

0.716 98 "J-(m'
Y

info 16 fioise O entnyay
.7 (a devours 0'1.

25. iteration

Cwy 1416
fj/ou 00111

scafi m mind

uyfoar/ (fie dioJ'C' ' amf
561116

downstream

0' 716 98 "J— (m'
Y

info 16 fioise O entnyay
'7 (a devours 0'11

26. iteration

wy 1416
fj/ou 00111

staff m mind

uyfoar/ (fie diOI'C' ' amf
561116

downstream

0' 716 98 "I7 (m'
Y

info 16 fioise O entnyay
'7 (a devours 0'11

29. iteration

**my 1416
fj/ou 00111**

staff In mind

**uyfoar/ (fie diOl'C' ' amf
561116**

downstream

**0' 716 98 "17(m'
Y**

**info 16fi0ise 0 entnyay
'7 (a devours 0'11**

30. iteration

**ml! 1416
lillllll llll111**

**uvloarl [lie llilll'fl' ' aml
561116**

**6' 116 98 "mm
Y**

**ill1015116156 ll Ellllww
'1 [a devours 6'11**

31. iteration

*ml! 1416
"HI" ||||111*

*uvloarl [lie Ililll'fl' ' aml
561116*

*6' 116 98 "mm
Y*

*i||1015116156 || E|||||WW
'1 [a devours 6'11*

32. iteration

***ml! 1416
"HI" ////111***

***uuloarl [lie llilll'fl' ' aml
561116***

***6116 98 "mm
Y***

***il /1015116156 // El / / / IWW
'1 [a devours 6'11***

33. iteration

ml! 1416
"HI" IIII111

uuloarl [lie IIiIII'fI' 'aml
561116

6116 98 "mm
Y

i! I1015116156 II El I I I IWW
'1 [a devours 6'11

34. iteration

ml! 1416
"H1"1111111

uuloarl [lie IIiIIIfl' 'aml
561116

6116 98 "mm
Y

i11101511615611E11111WW
'1 [a devours 6'11

41. iteration

ml.' 1416
"H1"1111111

uuloarl [lie //i\ \ \f' 'aml
561116

6116 98 "mm
Y

111101511615611E11111WW
'1 [a devours 6'11

44. iteration

mC ' 1416

"'1-(1 "1111111

uufom'f [fie //1{ f V" 'amf
561116

111101511615611511111 WW

'1 [a a(evours 6'11

62. iteration

**mews
"I70 "mm:**

**W 77 7 ow" M
56] 7 16**

IIIMIEIIfiIEfiIISIIII/'W

'I/éz ¢(zaam'a 67/

99. iteration

0 "mm:

7077 70m "7%
56 7779

\\\\\LL'(E\ ILIEILII LISLI \ ILINLI
W;Team;67/

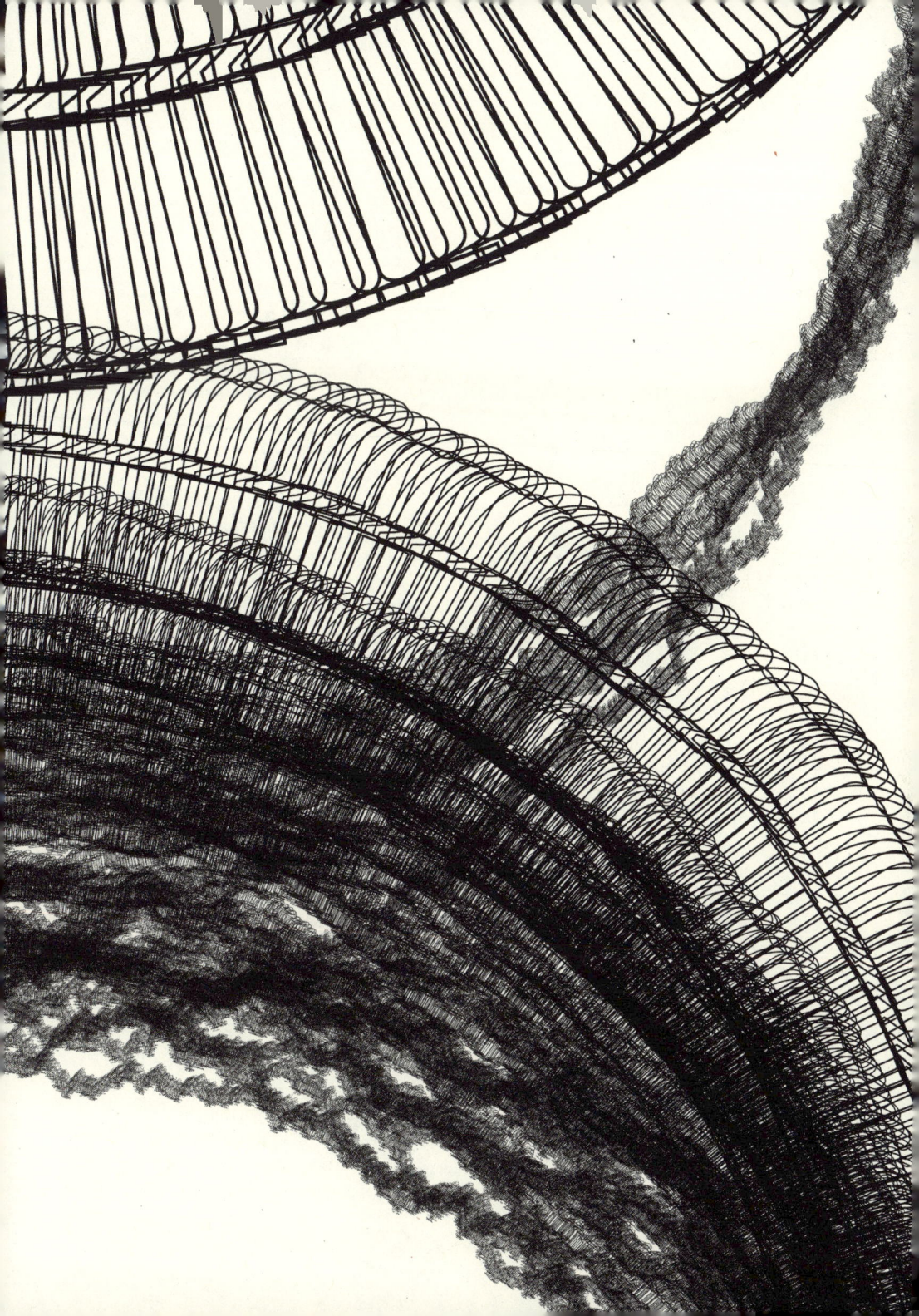

part of

eye is a part of needle.
eye is a part of visual system.
eye is a part of face.
face is a part of watch.
face is a part of ticker.
ticker is a part of circulatory system.
circulatory system is a part of body.
body is a part of organic structure.
body is a part of physical structure.
body is a part of narration.
body is a part of recital.
body is a part of yarn.
body is a part of address.
address is a part of letter.
letter is a part of correspondence.
letter is a part of mail.
letter is a part of spelling.
address is a part of missive.
missive is a part of correspondence.
missive is a part of mail.
body is a part of speech.
speech is a part of dialogue.
speech is a part of dialog.
speech is a part of paralanguage.
speech is a part of paralinguistic communication.
circulatory system is a part of organic structure.
circulatory system is a part of physical structure.
ticker is a part of cardiovascular system.
cardiovascular system is a part of body.
cardiovascular system is a part of organic structure.
cardiovascular system is a part of physical structure.
face is a part of playing card.
face is a part of head.
head is a part of drum.
drum is a part of drum brake.
head is a part of membranophone.
head is a part of tympan.
head is a part of nail.
nail is a part of integumentary system.
nail is a part of digit.
digit is a part of vertebrate.
digit is a part of craniate.
nail is a part of dactyl.
dactyl is a part of vertebrate.
dactyl is a part of craniate.
head is a part of screw.
screw is a part of ship.
screw is a part of outboard motor.
screw is a part of outboard.
head is a part of pin.
pin is a part of dinghy.
pin is a part of dory.
pin is a part of rowboat.
pin is a part of cylinder lock.
pin is a part of wrestling match.
head is a part of bolt.
bolt is a part of nut and bolt.
bolt is a part of lock.
lock is a part of gate.
gate is a part of air terminal.
air terminal is a part of airport.
air terminal is a part of airdrome.
air terminal is a part of aerodrome.
air terminal is a part of drome.
gate is a part of airport terminal.
airport terminal is a part of airport.
airport terminal is a part of airdrome.
airport terminal is a part of aerodrome.
airport terminal is a part of drome.

lock is a part of drawer.
drawer is a part of chest of drawers.
drawer is a part of chest.
chest is a part of torso.
torso is a part of body.
torso is a part of organic structure.
torso is a part of physical structure.
chest is a part of trunk.
trunk is a part of elephant.
trunk is a part of mammoth.
trunk is a part of car.
car is a part of cable railway.
car is a part of funicular.
car is a part of funicular railway.
car is a part of elevator.
elevator is a part of building.
elevator is a part of edifice.
elevator is a part of horizontal tail.
horizontal tail is a part of tail.
tail is a part of vertebrate.
tail is a part of craniate.
tail is a part of ship.
tail is a part of fuselage.
fuselage is a part of airplane.
fuselage is a part of aeroplane.
fuselage is a part of plane.
tail is a part of coin.
tail is a part of torso.
tail is a part of trunk.
trunk is a part of auto.
trunk is a part of automobile.
trunk is a part of machine.
trunk is a part of motorcar.
trunk is a part of body.
trunk is a part of organic structure.
trunk is a part of physical structure.
trunk is a part of tree.
tail is a part of body.
horizontal tail is a part of tail assembly.
tail assembly is a part of fuselage.
horizontal tail is a part of empennage.
empennage is a part of fuselage.
car is a part of lift.
lift is a part of building.
lift is a part of edifice.
lift is a part of heel.
heel is a part of shoe.
shoe is a part of drum brake.
heel is a part of boot.
heel is a part of golf-club head.
golf-club head is a part of golf club.
golf-club head is a part of golf-club.
golf-club head is a part of club.
heel is a part of club head.
club head is a part of golf club.
club head is a part of golf-club.
club head is a part of club.
heel is a part of club-head.
club-head is a part of golf club.
club-head is a part of golf-club.
club-head is a part of club.
heel is a part of clubhead.
clubhead is a part of golf club.
clubhead is a part of golf-club.
clubhead is a part of club.
heel is a part of foot.
foot is a part of invertebrate.
foot is a part of leg.
leg is a part of journey.
leg is a part of journeying.
leg is a part of trouser.
trouser is a part of pant.
leg is a part of pant.
leg is a part of table.
leg is a part of chair.
leg is a part of tripod.
leg is a part of spinning wheel.
leg is a part of grand piano.
leg is a part of grand.
leg is a part of hospital bed.
leg is a part of cot.
leg is a part of camp bed.

leg is a part of four-poster.
leg is a part of body.
leg is a part of organic structure.
leg is a part of physical structure.
leg is a part of furcation.
leg is a part of forking.
foot is a part of structure.
foot is a part of construction.
foot is a part of homo.
foot is a part of man.
man is a part of british isles.
british isles is a part of atlantic.
british isles is a part of atlantic ocean.
foot is a part of human being.
foot is a part of human.
foot is a part of yard.
yard is a part of sailing vessel.
yard is a part of sailing ship.
yard is a part of fathom.
yard is a part of fthm.
yard is a part of chain.
chain is a part of chain printer.
chain is a part of chain tongs.
chain is a part of bicycle.
chain is a part of bike.
chain is a part of wheel.
wheel is a part of steering system.
wheel is a part of steering mechanism.
wheel is a part of wheeled vehicle.
chain is a part of cycle.
cycle is a part of kilohertz.
kilohertz is a part of megahertz.
kilohertz is a part of mhz.
kilohertz is a part of megacycle per second.
kilohertz is a part of megacycle.
kilohertz is a part of mc.
cycle is a part of khz.
khz is a part of megahertz.
khz is a part of mhz.
khz is a part of megacycle per second.
khz is a part of megacycle.
khz is a part of mc.
cycle is a part of kilocycle per second.
kilocycle per second is a part of megahertz.
kilocycle per second is a part of mhz.
kilocycle per second is a part of megacycle per second.
kilocycle per second is a part of megacycle.
kilocycle per second is a part of mc.
cycle is a part of kilocycle.
kilocycle is a part of megahertz.
kilocycle is a part of mhz.
kilocycle is a part of megacycle per second.
kilocycle is a part of megacycle.
kilocycle is a part of mc.
cycle is a part of kc.
kc is a part of megahertz.
kc is a part of mhz.
kc is a part of megacycle per second.
kc is a part of megacycle.
kc is a part of mc.
chain is a part of molecule.
yard is a part of perch.
perch is a part of roost.
perch is a part of yellow perch.
perch is a part of perca flavescens.
perch is a part of european perch.
perch is a part of perca fluviatilis.
perch is a part of furlong.
furlong is a part of mile.
mile is a part of league.
furlong is a part of statute mile.
statute mile is a part of league.
furlong is a part of stat mi.
stat mi is a part of league.
furlong is a part of land mile.
land mile is a part of league.
furlong is a part of international mile.
international mile is a part of league.

furlong is a part of mi.
mi is a part of united states.
united states is a part of north america.
north america is a part of western hemisphere.
north america is a part of occident.
north america is a part of new world.
north america is a part of west.
west is a part of united states.
west is a part of united states of america.
united states of america is a part of north america.
north america is a part of northern hemisphere.
north america is a part of america.
america is a part of north america.
west is a part of america.
west is a part of the states.
the states is a part of north america.
west is a part of us.
us is a part of north america.
west is a part of u.s..
u.s. is a part of north america.
west is a part of usa.
usa is a part of department of defense.
usa is a part of defense department.
usa is a part of united states department of defense.
usa is a part of defense.
defense is a part of trial.
usa is a part of dod.
usa is a part of north america.
west is a part of u.s.a..
u.s.a. is a part of north america.
mi is a part of united states of america.
mi is a part of america.
mi is a part of the states.
mi is a part of us.
mi is a part of u.s..
mi is a part of usa.
mi is a part of u.s.a..
mi is a part of midwest.
midwest is a part of united states.
midwest is a part of united states of america.
midwest is a part of america.
midwest is a part of the states.
midwest is a part of us.
midwest is a part of u.s..
midwest is a part of usa.
midwest is a part of u.s.a..
mi is a part of middle west.
middle west is a part of united states.
middle west is a part of united states of america.
middle west is a part of america.
middle west is a part of the states.
middle west is a part of us.
middle west is a part of u.s..
middle west is a part of usa.
middle west is a part of u.s.a..
mi is a part of midwestern united states.
midwestern united states is a part of united states.
midwestern united states is a part of united states of america.
midwestern united states is a part of america.
midwestern united states is a part of the states.
midwestern united states is a part of us.
midwestern united states is a part of u.s..
midwestern united states is a part of usa.
midwestern united states is a part of u.s.a..
mi is a part of league.

mi is a part of heart attack.
yard is a part of rod.
rod is a part of retina.
retina is a part of eye.
eye is a part of human face.
human face is a part of head.
head is a part of hammer.
hammer is a part of piano action.
piano action is a part of piano.
piano action is a part of pianoforte.
piano action is a part of forte-piano.
hammer is a part of gunlock.
gunlock is a part of gun.
gun is a part of car.
car is a part of airship.
car is a part of dirigible.
gun is a part of auto.
gun is a part of automobile.
gun is a part of machine.
gun is a part of motorcar.
gun is a part of airplane.
gun is a part of aeroplane.
gun is a part of plane.
gun is a part of battery.
battery is a part of baseball team.
hammer is a part of firing mechanism.
firing mechanism is a part of gun.
hammer is a part of percussion instrument.
hammer is a part of percussive instrument.
hammer is a part of middle ear.
middle ear is a part of auditory apparatus.
auditory apparatus is a part of auditory system.
hammer is a part of tympanic cavity.
tympanic cavity is a part of auditory apparatus.
hammer is a part of tympanum.
tympanum is a part of ear.

ear is a part of head.
head is a part of ram.
head is a part of coin.
head is a part of skeletal muscle.
head is a part of striated muscle.
head is a part of body.
head is a part of organic structure.
head is a part of physical structure.
head is a part of animal.
head is a part of animate being.
head is a part of beast.
head is a part of brute.
head is a part of creature.
head is a part of fauna.
head is a part of arrow.
arrow is a part of bow and arrow.
head is a part of pointer.
head is a part of abscess.
ear is a part of caput.
caput is a part of body.
caput is a part of organic structure.
caput is a part of physical structure.
caput is a part of animal.
caput is a part of animate being.
caput is a part of beast.
caput is a part of brute.
caput is a part of creature.
caput is a part of fauna.
ear is a part of auditory system.
ear is a part of vestibular apparatus.
ear is a part of vestibular system.
ear is a part of external ear.
external ear is a part of auditory apparatus.
ear is a part of outer ear.
outer ear is a part of auditory apparatus.
ear is a part of corn.
corn is a part of maize.
corn is a part of indian corn.
corn is a part of zea mays.
ear is a part of maize.

ear is a part of indian corn.
ear is a part of zea mays.
tympanum is a part of auditory apparatus.
human face is a part of caput.
human face is a part of homo.
human face is a part of man.
human face is a part of human being.
human face is a part of human.
retina is a part of oculus.
oculus is a part of visual system.
oculus is a part of face.
face is a part of racket.
face is a part of racquet.
face is a part of golf-club head.
face is a part of club head.
face is a part of club-head.
face is a part of clubhead.
face is a part of caput.
face is a part of homo.
face is a part of man.
face is a part of human being.
face is a part of human.
face is a part of animal.
face is a part of animate being.
face is a part of beast.
face is a part of brute.
face is a part of creature.
face is a part of fauna.
oculus is a part of human face.
retina is a part of optic.
optic is a part of visual system.
optic is a part of face.
optic is a part of human face.
rod is a part of furlong.
yard is a part of pole.
pole is a part of magnet.
pole is a part of electrical device.
pole is a part of battery.
pole is a part of electric battery.
pole is a part of furlong.
yard is a part of lea.

lea is a part of country.
lea is a part of rural area.
foot is a part of pace.
pace is a part of walk.
pace is a part of walking.
pace is a part of fathom.
pace is a part of fthm.
pace is a part of chain.
pace is a part of perch.
pace is a part of rod.
pace is a part of pole.
pace is a part of lea.
heel is a part of human foot.
human foot is a part of leg.
human foot is a part of homo.
human foot is a part of man.
human foot is a part of human being.
human foot is a part of human.
heel is a part of pes.
pes is a part of leg.
pes is a part of homo.
pes is a part of man.
pes is a part of human being.
pes is a part of human.
heel is a part of loaf of bread.
heel is a part of loaf.
chest is a part of body.
chest is a part of vertebrate.
chest is a part of craniate.
chest is a part of thorax.
thorax is a part of insect.
thorax is a part of torso.
thorax is a part of trunk.
thorax is a part of body.
thorax is a part of vertebrate.
thorax is a part of craniate.
thorax is a part of arthropod.
chest is a part of pectus.
pectus is a part of torso.
pectus is a part of trunk.
pectus is a part of body.
pectus is a part of vertebrate.

pectus is a part of craniate.
drawer is a part of bureau.
drawer is a part of dresser.
drawer is a part of buffet.
buffet is a part of dining room.
dining room is a part of dwelling.
dining room is a part of home.
dining room is a part of domicile.
dining room is a part of abode.
dining room is a part of habitation.
dining room is a part of dwelling house.
buffet is a part of dining-room.
dining-room is a part of dwelling.
dining-room is a part of home.
dining-room is a part of domicile.
dining-room is a part of abode.
dining-room is a part of habitation.
dining-room is a part of dwelling house.
drawer is a part of counter.
counter is a part of dining room.
counter is a part of dining-room.
counter is a part of shoe.
counter is a part of boot.
drawer is a part of sideboard.
sideboard is a part of dining room.
sideboard is a part of dining-room.
drawer is a part of chiffonier.
drawer is a part of commode.
commode is a part of toilet.
toilet is a part of lavatory.
toilet is a part of lav.
toilet is a part of can.
can is a part of toilet.
toilet is a part of john.
john is a part of new testament.
new testament is a part of bible.
new testament is a part of christian bible.
new testament is a part of book.
book is a part of text.
text is a part of publication.
text is a part of bible.
text is a part of christian bible.
text is a part of book.
book is a part of textual matter.
textual matter is a part of publication.
text is a part of good book.
text is a part of holy scripture.
text is a part of holy writ.
text is a part of scripture.
text is a part of word of god.
text is a part of word.
word is a part of kilobyte.
kilobyte is a part of megabyte.
megabyte is a part of gigabyte.
gigabyte is a part of terabyte.
terabyte is a part of petabyte.
petabyte is a part of exabyte.
exabyte is a part of zettabyte.
zettabyte is a part of yottabyte.
zettabyte is a part of yobibyte.
zettabyte is a part of yb.
zettabyte is a part of yib.
exabyte is a part of zebibyte.
zebibyte is a part of yottabyte.
zebibyte is a part of yobibyte.
zebibyte is a part of yb.
zebibyte is a part of yib.
exabyte is a part of zb.
zb is a part of yottabyte.
zb is a part of yobibyte.
zb is a part of yb.
zb is a part of yib.
zb is a part of yottabit.
zb is a part of ybit.
exabyte is a part of zib.
zib is a part of yottabyte.
zib is a part of yobibyte.
zib is a part of yb.
zib is a part of yib.
petabyte is a part of exbibyte.

exbibyte is a part of zettabyte.
exbibyte is a part of zebibyte.
exbibyte is a part of zb.
exbibyte is a part of zib.
petabyte is a part of eb.
eb is a part of zettabyte.
eb is a part of zebibyte.
eb is a part of zb.
eb is a part of zib.
eb is a part of zettabit.
zettabit is a part of yottabit.
zettabit is a part of ybit.
zettabit is a part of yb.
eb is a part of zbit.
zbit is a part of yottabit.
zbit is a part of ybit.
zbit is a part of yb.
petabyte is a part of eib.
eib is a part of zettabyte.
eib is a part of zebibyte.
eib is a part of zb.
eib is a part of zib.
terabyte is a part of pebibyte.
pebibyte is a part of exabyte.
pebibyte is a part of exbibyte.
pebibyte is a part of eb.
pebibyte is a part of eib.
terabyte is a part of pb.
pb is a part of exabyte.
pb is a part of exbibyte.
pb is a part of eb.
pb is a part of eib.
pb is a part of exabit.
exabit is a part of zettabit.
exabit is a part of zbit.
exabit is a part of zb.
pb is a part of ebit.
ebit is a part of zettabit.
ebit is a part of zbit.
ebit is a part of zb.
terabyte is a part of pib.
pib is a part of exabyte.

pib is a part of exbibyte.
pib is a part of eb.
pib is a part of eib.
gigabyte is a part of tebibyte.
tebibyte is a part of petabyte.
tebibyte is a part of pebibyte.
tebibyte is a part of pb.
tebibyte is a part of pib.
gigabyte is a part of tb.
tb is a part of petabyte.
tb is a part of pebibyte.
tb is a part of pb.
tb is a part of pib.
tb is a part of petabit.
petabit is a part of exabit.
petabit is a part of ebit.
petabit is a part of eb.
tb is a part of pbit.
pbit is a part of exabit.
pbit is a part of ebit.
pbit is a part of eb.
gigabyte is a part of tib.
tib is a part of petabyte.
tib is a part of pebibyte.
tib is a part of pb.
tib is a part of pib.
megabyte is a part of gibibyte.
gibibyte is a part of terabyte.
gibibyte is a part of tebibyte.
gibibyte is a part of tb.
gibibyte is a part of tib.
megabyte is a part of g.
g is a part of law of gravitation.
law of gravitation is a part of theory of gravitation.
law of gravitation is a part of theory of gravity.
law of gravitation is a part of gravitational theory.
law of gravitation is a part of newton.
newton is a part of sthene.

g is a part of newton.
g is a part of terabyte.
g is a part of tebibyte.
g is a part of tb.
g is a part of tib.
g is a part of dekagram.
dekagram is a part of hectogram.
hectogram is a part of kilogram.
kilogram is a part of myriagram.
myriagram is a part of centner.
centner is a part of short ton.
short ton is a part of kiloton.
kiloton is a part of megaton.
centner is a part of ton.
ton is a part of kiloton.
centner is a part of net ton.
net ton is a part of kiloton.
centner is a part of hundredweight.
hundredweight is a part of long ton.
hundredweight is a part of ton.
hundredweight is a part of gross ton.
hundredweight is a part of short ton.
hundredweight is a part of net ton.
hundredweight is a part of quintal.
quintal is a part of short ton.
quintal is a part of ton.
quintal is a part of net ton.
quintal is a part of metric ton.
quintal is a part of mt.
mt is a part of united states.
mt is a part of united states of america.
mt is a part of america.
mt is a part of the states.
mt is a part of us.
mt is a part of u.s..
mt is a part of usa.
mt is a part of u.s.a..
quintal is a part of tonne.
quintal is a part of t.
centner is a part of metric hundredweight.
metric hundredweight is a part of quintal.
centner is a part of doppelzentner.
doppelzentner is a part of quintal.
centner is a part of quintal.
kilogram is a part of myg.
myg is a part of centner.
hectogram is a part of kg.
kg is a part of myriagram.
kg is a part of myg.
hectogram is a part of kilo.
kilo is a part of myriagram.
kilo is a part of myg.
dekagram is a part of hg.
hg is a part of kilogram.
hg is a part of kg.
hg is a part of kilo.
g is a part of decagram.
decagram is a part of hectogram.
decagram is a part of hg.
g is a part of dkg.
dkg is a part of hectogram.
dkg is a part of hg.
g is a part of dag.
dag is a part of garment.
dag is a part of hectogram.
dag is a part of hg.
megabyte is a part of gb.
gb is a part of british isles.
gb is a part of terabyte.
gb is a part of tebibyte.
gb is a part of tb.
gb is a part of tib.
gb is a part of terabit.
terabit is a part of petabit.
terabit is a part of pbit.
terabit is a part of pb.
gb is a part of tbit.
tbit is a part of petabit.
tbit is a part of pbit.
tbit is a part of pb.
megabyte is a part of gib.

gib is a part of terabyte.
gib is a part of tebibyte.
gib is a part of tb.
gib is a part of tib.
kilobyte is a part of mebibyte.
mebibyte is a part of gigabyte.
mebibyte is a part of gibibyte.
mebibyte is a part of g.
mebibyte is a part of gb.
mebibyte is a part of gib.
kilobyte is a part of m.
m is a part of gigabyte.
m is a part of gibibyte.
m is a part of g.
m is a part of gb.
m is a part of gib.
m is a part of decameter.
decameter is a part of hectometer.
hectometer is a part of kilometer.
kilometer is a part of myriameter.
kilometer is a part of myriametre.
kilometer is a part of mym.
hectometer is a part of kilometre.
kilometre is a part of myriameter.
kilometre is a part of myriametre.
kilometre is a part of mym.
hectometer is a part of km.
km is a part of myriameter.
km is a part of myriametre.
km is a part of mym.
hectometer is a part of klick.
klick is a part of myriameter.
klick is a part of myriametre.
klick is a part of mym.
decameter is a part of hectometre.
hectometre is a part of kilometer.
hectometre is a part of kilometre.
hectometre is a part of km.
hectometre is a part of klick.
decameter is a part of hm.
hm is a part of kilometer.
hm is a part of kilometre.
hm is a part of km.
hm is a part of klick.
m is a part of dekameter.
dekameter is a part of hectometer.
dekameter is a part of hectometre.
dekameter is a part of hm.
m is a part of decametre.
decametre is a part of hectometer.
decametre is a part of hectometre.
decametre is a part of hm.
m is a part of dekametre.
dekametre is a part of hectometer.
dekametre is a part of hectometre.
dekametre is a part of hm.
m is a part of dam.
dam is a part of hectometer.
dam is a part of hectometre.
dam is a part of hm.
m is a part of dkm.
dkm is a part of hectometer.
dkm is a part of hectometre.
dkm is a part of hm.
kilobyte is a part of mb.
mb is a part of gigabyte.
mb is a part of gibibyte.
mb is a part of g.
mb is a part of gb.
mb is a part of gib.
mb is a part of gigabit.
gigabit is a part of terabit.
gigabit is a part of tbit.
gigabit is a part of tb.
mb is a part of gbit.
gbit is a part of terabit.
gbit is a part of tbit.
gbit is a part of tb.
kilobyte is a part of mib.
mib is a part of gigabyte.
mib is a part of gibibyte.
mib is a part of g.
mib is a part of gb.
mib is a part of gib.

word is a part of kibibyte.
kibibyte is a part of megabyte.
kibibyte is a part of mebibyte.
kibibyte is a part of m.
kibibyte is a part of mb.
kibibyte is a part of mib.
word is a part of k.
k is a part of megabyte.
k is a part of mebibyte.
k is a part of m.
k is a part of mb.
k is a part of mib.
word is a part of kb.
kb is a part of megabyte.
kb is a part of mebibyte.
kb is a part of m.
kb is a part of mb.
kb is a part of mib.
kb is a part of megabit.
megabit is a part of gigabit.
megabit is a part of gbit.
megabit is a part of gb.
kb is a part of mbit.
mbit is a part of gigabit.
mbit is a part of gbit.
mbit is a part of gb.
word is a part of kib.
kib is a part of megabyte.
kib is a part of mebibyte.
kib is a part of m.
kib is a part of mb.
kib is a part of mib.
new testament is a part of good book.
new testament is a part of holy scripture.
new testament is a part of holy writ.
new testament is a part of scripture.
new testament is a part of word of god.
new testament is a part of word.
toilet is a part of privy.
toilet is a part of bathroom.
bathroom is a part of dwelling.
bathroom is a part of home.
bathroom is a part of domicile.
bathroom is a part of abode.
bathroom is a part of habitation.
bathroom is a part of dwelling house.
toilet is a part of bath.
bath is a part of dwelling.
bath is a part of home.
bath is a part of domicile.
bath is a part of abode.
bath is a part of habitation.
bath is a part of dwelling house.
bath is a part of bathroom.
bath is a part of england.
england is a part of united kingdom.
united kingdom is a part of british isles.
england is a part of uk.
uk is a part of british isles.
england is a part of u.k..
u.k. is a part of british isles.
england is a part of britain.
britain is a part of british isles.
england is a part of united kingdom of great britain and northern ireland.
united kingdom of great britain and northern ireland is a part of british isles.
england is a part of great britain.
great britain is a part of british isles.
england is a part of europe.
europe is a part of eurasia.
eurasia is a part of eastern hemisphere.
eurasia is a part of orient.
eurasia is a part of northern hemisphere.
europe is a part of west.
europe is a part of occident.
bath is a part of homer.

bath is a part of kor.
can is a part of lavatory.
can is a part of lav.
can is a part of john.
can is a part of privy.
can is a part of bathroom.
can is a part of bath.
can is a part of torso.
can is a part of trunk.
can is a part of body.
commode is a part of lavatory.
commode is a part of lav.
commode is a part of can.
commode is a part of john.
commode is a part of privy.
commode is a part of bathroom.
commode is a part of bath.
drawer is a part of desk.
lock is a part of door.
door is a part of doorway.
doorway is a part of wall.
wall is a part of fortification.
wall is a part of munition.
wall is a part of building.
wall is a part of edifice.
wall is a part of room.
room is a part of building.
room is a part of edifice.
wall is a part of hallway.
wall is a part of hall.
hall is a part of building.
hall is a part of edifice.
hall is a part of mansion.
mansion is a part of zodiac.
zodiac is a part of celestial sphere.
zodiac is a part of sphere.
zodiac is a part of empyrean.
zodiac is a part of firmament.
zodiac is a part of heavens.
zodiac is a part of vault of heaven.
zodiac is a part of welkin.
hall is a part of mansion house.
hall is a part of manse.
hall is a part of residence.
wall is a part of cave.
door is a part of room access.
room access is a part of wall.
door is a part of threshold.
threshold is a part of doorway.
threshold is a part of door.
door is a part of wall.
threshold is a part of room access.
threshold is a part of wall.
lock is a part of lid.
lid is a part of box.
box is a part of balcony.
box is a part of coach.
box is a part of four-in-hand.
box is a part of coach-and-four.
box is a part of ball field.
ball field is a part of ballpark.
ball field is a part of park.
park is a part of urban area.
park is a part of populated area.
box is a part of baseball field.
baseball field is a part of ballpark.
baseball field is a part of park.
box is a part of diamond.
diamond is a part of ballpark.
diamond is a part of park.
diamond is a part of ball field.
diamond is a part of baseball field.
lid is a part of chest.
lid is a part of jar.
lid is a part of eye.
lid is a part of oculus.
lid is a part of optic.
lock is a part of ignition switch.
ignition switch is a part of ignition.
ignition is a part of electrical system.
electrical system is a part of motor vehicle.
electrical system is a part of automotive vehicle.

ignition switch is a part of ignition system.
ignition system is a part of electrical system.
lock is a part of canal.
lock is a part of firearm.
lock is a part of piece.
piece is a part of unit.
piece is a part of building block.
lock is a part of small-arm.
lock is a part of hairdo.
lock is a part of hairstyle.
lock is a part of hair style.
lock is a part of coiffure.
lock is a part of coif.
bolt is a part of rifle.

andandandand...

text

text twixt taxed taxer taxi taxy
toxa taxite taxeme taxis taxon taxor
texan texas toxic twixt text taxi
taxite taxis toxic toxin taxy thixle
toxa ptyxis taxine taxed taxer taxon
taxed taxer taxeme taxi taxy taxine
taxis taxite taxon taxor text toxa
toxoid tacso taxus taxer taxed taxor
taxeme taxi taxy taxine taxis taxite
taxon text toxa tagsore tacso taxus
taxi taxis taxy taxine taxite taxed
taxer taxon taxor toxa toxic toxin
text twixt ptyxis taxy taxi taxed
taxer taxis taxon taxor toxa text
taxeme taxine taxite tacso taxus toxic
toxa taxi taxy toxic toxin toxon
taxon taxor text taxed taxer taxis
toxoid toxone texan taxite taxine taxi
taxis taxed taxeme taxer twixt taxy
text thixle taxon taxor toxic toxin
taxeme taxed taxer taxine taxite taxi
taxy taxis taxon taxor text toxa
toxone thioxene thixle taxis taxi ptyxis
taxine taxite taxy taxed taxer taxon
taxor taxus toxic toxin tacso takosis
taxon taxor toxon taxi taxine taxy
toxin toxone taxed taxer taxis toxa
tacso taxeme taxite taxor taxer taxon
taxi taxy taxed taxis toxa toxon
tacso tagsore taxeme taxine taxite text
texan texas taxon taxus text toxa
taxi taxy toxin toxon taxine texas
texan taxus taxis text toxa taxi
taxy tagassu tagish toxic toxin taxi
toxa toxoid taxis toxon twixt ptyxis
taxine taxite taxon taxor taxy text

will have been

all was in vain a year ago.
we are correct in this moment.
nothing will be like it was in a few minutes.
the day before yesterday we were ready for anything.
now nothing is like it was.
in a few minutes we will have been correct.
all was worse a week ago.
we are ready for anything today.
currently all is better.
just now we were overcautious.
we will be overcautious tomorrow.
the day after tomorrow it will have been all the same to us.
in a month all will be in vain.
we will have been happy very soon.
last month all was better.
all is in vain currently.
we were correct yesterday.
in this moment we are happy.
now we are overcautious.
in a year we will have been ready for anything.
it is all the same to us today.
nothing was like it was last month.
all will have been better in the future.
a year ago we were careless.
all is worse in this moment.
we were unexperienced a week ago.
we will have been unexperienced in a week.
just now it was all the same to us.
in a few minutes all will have been worse.
currently we are unexperienced.

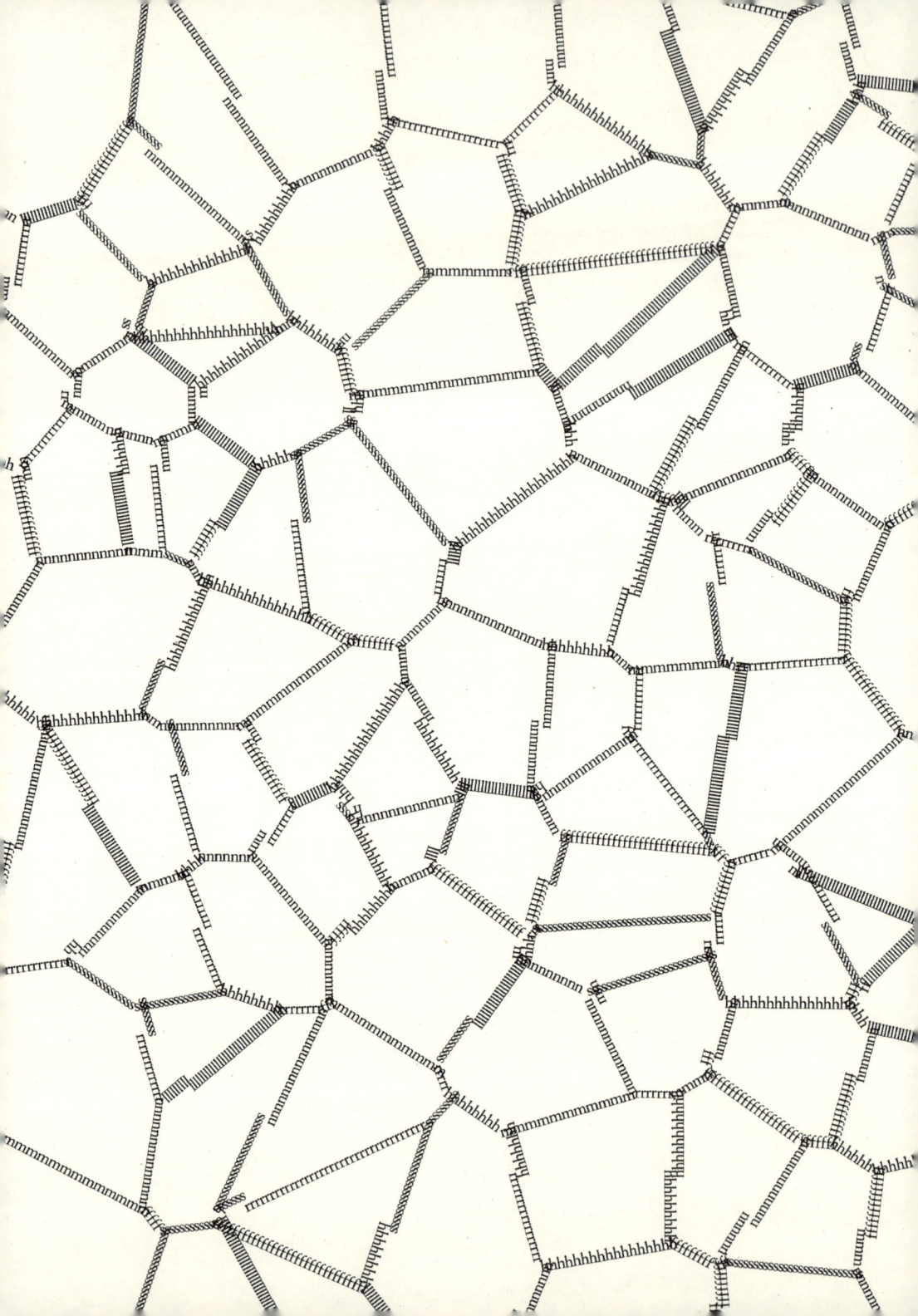

pots	**post**	ptos	ptso
psot	psto	**opts**	opst
otps	otsp	ospt	ostp
tpos	tpso	**tops**	tosp
tspo	tsop	**spot**	spto
sopt	sotp	stpo	**stop**

paratext

method

a project like this book needs a different approach than any other literary publication. instead of typing text into a word processing app i created programs, searched for usable data, converted it into material the programs could work with, trained artificial neural networks, skimmed text corpora and corrected bugs and errors in my programs.

the main part of this book was not written in german or english but in programming languages like c++, lua, objective c, lisp, python, clojure, prolog and haskell. i only hand-typed the explanations and the other paratexts, all literary text was generated by the programs i wrote.

in a normal book you can see all work done except for deleted parts and changes in print whereas in this book most of the written text stays hidden on my hard disc. the programs and moreso the data used would fill many volumes and still only be readable for an expert audience.

for me as an author programming those texts was not always paired with instant gratification. for example training a neural network with textual data sometimes took hours or days and then in the end did not produce the results i was interested in.

this way of working often resembled the tasks of gardening: sow. wait. unexpected results. sow again. wait. be disappointed or astonished...

translating data poetry

i am in no way a professional translator, so why did i choose to translate the german *datenpoesie* texts into english myself?

in order to stick to the concept of the computer generated data poetry, i had to translate the programs that generated the texts rather than the texts themselves. so it turned out to be more of a programming task than a literary translation.

for each of the programs, i first had to decide if an english version was at all possible. german and english share common roots but of course differ greatly in expressions, vocabulary and idioms. however, my programs don't depend very much on subtleties or precise expressions, so most of the time it was not too hard to transfer the concepts. but in some cases, idiosyncracies of the german language (such as compound words) prohibited a meaningful translation.

depending on the structure of the program, translating from german to english was not too complicated as english grammar is simpler and has less need for grammatical congruency between words. the more challenging task was to find translated or equivalent data the programs could operate on. linguistic data or large text corpora were often available in german and english but for smaller and more specific source texts, i had to find a translated version.
also, in some cases rather than translated texts i chose to use cultural equivalents, or rather, personal preferences. for example, instead of matthias claudius' "abendlied" i selected william wordsworth's "i wandered lonely as a cloud" or instead of heinrich heine's collected poems, i took walt whitman's.

the poems depending on automatic translation services were very easy to translate as often only a change in the specification of the output language was required, such as in the kanji-texts, where i instructed the program to translate the japanese source text into english instead of german.

in only one case, i decided not to modify the program at all but to use an automatic translator to convert the result of the generated german text into english: the grammar that creates the random wittgenstein imitation was too hard and too boring to translate into english, so i took this shortcut.

thanks
to lisa rosenblatt for helping me to find some of the flaws in this book. all remaining problems are my fault alone.

explanations and comments

page 4: a beginning

a formal grammar generates a random constellation of chained definitions. the program begins at the symbol START and replaces it with SENTENCE. the symbol SENTENCE is then substituted with the rule's content and so on. the symbol | denotes random choices the algorithm can make. capitalized symbols are substituted by the rule's content whereas lowercase characters are copied into the results without any substitution. the rules of the formal grammar:

START → SENTENCE
CHOSENSUBJECT → a beginning
VERB → is
SENTENCE → CHOSENSUBJECT VERB OBJECT.
OBJECT → {CHOSENSUBJECT:SUBJECT} CHOSENSUBJECT
SUBJECT → SUBJECTS | ADJSUBJECT | ADJSUBJECT | ADJSUBJECT
ADJSUBJECT → a ADJSSTEM SUBJECTS
ADJSSTEM → simple | fast | slow | soft | hard | dark | light | small | huge | cheap | valuable | lazy | hot | cold | new | dated | smart | dumb
SUBJECTS → a SUBJECTS2
SUBJECTS2 → hand | tongue | desparation | malady | darkness | light | community | warmth | survey | collection | wall | coldness | splendor | power | sentence | meaning | start | doubt | death | success | word | heart | conclusion | hope | desire | fire | face | wish | finger | reward | point | closeness

page 5: i want to write a book

this text was written by the software GPT-2 that caused a stir in february 2019 when the developers published examples of human-like texts written by it. this text was generated with a limited version of the software starting with the writing prompt "i want to write a book that". the full version of GPT-2 has not been published yet due to fear of misuse.

page 7: chains
the program searches for word lists in which the words are constructed by adding a letter to the previous word.

pages 9–10: portmanteau
portmanteau words are artifical words consisting of two or more amalgamized words. the words in this text are constructed automatically by a search in my word database.

page 11: traces
the image is generated by the simulation of the movements of a flock of birds according to three simple rules first formulated by craig reynolds in 1986:
- each actor (in my case letter) tries to keep a certain distance from the other actors.
- each one tries to follow the mean direction of the movement of the flock.
- each one tries not to fly too far away swarm.

these three rules create a complex pattern that resembles the movement of flocks or swarms of animals.

pages 12–13: proverbs
a collection of proverbs is analyzed and resynthesized by markov chains.

page 14: kanji I
from a list of the 44 most common japanese kanji (ideogrammatic signs) four

are chosen and permutated. the resulting pseudo-japanese text is translated automatically into english.

page 28: occupations
each sentence is translated into turkish and back into english by a commercial automatic translator. some personal pronouns in turkish are gender neutral, so the translator service has to choose a new gender when translating back from the turkish phrase. in some cases, the text reveals a bias that stems from the data with which the translation algorithm was trained.

page 29: seasons
a generative grammar creates four short poems.

page 31: the word
the words of walt whitman's poems are ordered into clusters. the program searches for the cluster that includes the words "the word" and uses the other words in the cluster for another search for clusters. it then takes the first four words of each newly found cluster as a line of the poem.

page 33: natural language — property
generation of sentences in natural language on the topic of property and its desired exchange.

page 35: natural language — maslow's hierarchy of needs
generation of natural language based on maslow's hierarchy of needs. what do humans need? the computer knows.

page 37: natural language — random epigraphs
random verbs, nouns and adjectives are combined in a grammatically correct manner for enigmatic epigraphs.

page 39: word frequency
starting with the wikipedia article for "word", a list of words that appear only once in the article is created. fifty of those words are each again the topic of a new search in wikipedia. the found articles are stored in a text corpus and its most common and most rare words are then combined to form the lines of the poem.

page 41: yesterday
a formal grammar generates sentences.

pages 43–44: subtitle
the algorithm searches in a corpus of movie subtitles for the phrases "i thought", "she thought", "i asked", "she said", "she asked" and "i said" and arranges the found sentences. the data was retrieved from opensubtitles.org

pages 45–46: captions
a computer program (neuraltalk2) watches me through the laptop camera as i walk up and down my studio, receive phone calls, wave at the camera and so on. the program tries to describe what it sees.

pages 48–49: line by line
an artifical neural network that usually translates phrases from one language into another is trained with lines of dialogues taken from a corpus of movie subtitles. the network learns how to answer a starting line with a consecutive

line. the result is then used for a new "translation" and so on. this creates surreal dialogues.

page 52: what is
a search on twitter for the phrase "what is". the found questions are then searched on twitter and the results are arranged behind the question.

pages 54–55: if i
a search on twitter for the phrase "if i".

pages 57–58: interests
what could be of interest? an internet search reveals the answers.

pages 60–64: nations
a search on twitter for the phrases "usa is", "canada is", "uk is", "australia is" and "new zealand is". the results are analyzed with linguistic methods and filtered for adjectives. the most common adjectives in the searchs results are larger and the least common ones smaller.

pages 69–70: univers declar human right
the *universal declaration of human rights* is treated by the same process that search engines use to extract relevant information from a website. they first remove unimportant words (or so called stop words) and then reduce all words to their word stem.

page 72: artificial unintelligence
a neural network (multi-layer recurrent neural network) is trained with the beginning of adolf hitler's *mein kampf* in english translation. the network then

generates this text automatically.

page 73: XY
two unstable towers consisting of the characters X and Y fall into each other. the process is calculated by a physics simulation.

page 74: tale I
fairy tales by the brothers grimm are analyzed and resynthesized by a markov chain.

page 76: tale II
fairy tales by the brothers grimm are analyzed and resynthesized by a markov chain.

page 78: suggestion for the next few weeks
a text generated by the word-suggestion function of a smartphone.

pages 80–81: populist fable I
the text is generated by one of the oldest narrative text generators, talespin by james meehan. orginally, the generator created aesopian fables. my version transfers the setting into the world of today but keeps the language as well as the characters simple.

page 83: uncertainty
a complex generative grammar extracted from sentences and phrases from ludwig wittgenstein's *über gewissheit (on certainty)* creates a german text. since translating the german grammar into an english generative grammar would be extremely complicated, i decided to use an automatic translator service to

translate the generated german text into english.

page 85: most common words
the program chooses randomly from a list of the 100 most common english words. this creates an almost readable text.

pages 87–88: anagrams
anagrams with a word length of five are filtered from the word list.

page 90: word squares 4x4
word squares modelled after the latin sator-square. created by an exhaustive automatic search in my word database.

pages 92–99: ators ate
a search in a wordlist for word-pairs that end with "ators" and "ate" but share the same prefix.

pages 101–106: decay
a poem is saved as an image. then a character recognition program converts it back into textual information. after 99 repetitions of this process, the text has disappeared. the program and the idea is based on a program by the artist mouse reeve: mousereeve.com

pages 108–120: part of
a database of word relations (wordnet) is explored beginning with the word "eye". the program then follows the part-of relation and exhausts all possibilities.

page 122: text
a spellchecking algorithm searches for words similar to the word "text" and arranges them in lines of five.

page 123: will have been
a generative grammar writes sentences with a specific or vague time designation.

page 125: stop
all permutations of the characters of the word "stop".

glossary

algorithm
an algorithm is a distinct instruction for the solution of a problem. a common example would be the recipe for how to cook a soft-boiled egg (cook the egg for 4 minutes and 45 seconds) or the instructions for how to divide two numbers by hand on paper.

artificial intelligence
artificial intelligence is a term for numerous attempts to automate a range of intelligent behavior or learning. it encompasses many different fields such as knowledge based systems, pattern recognition, pattern prediction, robotics and artificial life. the ambitious goals that were proclaimed in the 1960s have not been reached. however, in recent years, interest has again grown massively due to the increased power of computers that make new and better applications possible.

character recognition
character recognition is the automatic recognition of text in images and is used to convert scanned images to text documents.

corpus
a text corpus is a collection of text data in a certain language. a parallel corpus is a body of text that is available in different languages as translations, such as the protocols of the european parliament.

c++
c++ is a widespread programming language that is used universally. it offers high execution speed as well as a high degree of abstraction. the name itself is a program and a self referential joke. the expression c++ instructs the computer to increase the value of the variable c (c was the name of the precursor of c++) by one.

formal grammar
a formal grammar is a formal system that consists of a start symbol and rules. the rules describe how certain symbols can be substituted with other symbols that can again be replaced. a system like this can model and create complex texts.

kabbalah
the kabbalah is a mystical tradition that originates in judaism. it enables the scholar to make simple calculations based on values derived from words and gain religious insights through them.

lisp
lisp is one of the first programming languages (1958) and the second oldest that is still in wide use. it offers high flexibility and was used early on to experiment with artificial intelligence concepts.

lua
lua is a programming language that can be incorporated easily into other programs to make them more flexible.

markov chain
a markov chain can be used to predict future events by analyzing a history of events. applied to text they use the probabilities of character sequences. for example, the algorithm calculates how likely it would be that the prefix "im" is followed by the letter "p" or "m" in a a given text. analyzing the whole text in this way results in a probability table that can then be used to resynthesize a text that resembles the original text to a certain degree.

natural language
the term natural language is used in computer linguistics for human language in general (contrary to computer or formal languages).

neural network
an artificial neural network is a simplified simulation of natural neural networks and is used in artificial intelligence systems to create unsupervised learning programs and pattern recognition.

permutation
permutation is the rearrangement of objects in a certain order. in this book i use the term as a synonym for "permutation without repetition", which specifies that objects should occur only once.

physics simulation
a physics simulation is a program that simulates physical laws. in my case, the simulation models the laws of newtonian physics that can be observed in

everyday life. it mainly simulates gravity, friction, inertia and reflection of objects.

python
python is a universal and widely used programming language. it is often used for natural language processing and artificial intelligence.

recurrent neural network
a recurrent neural network is a neural network that can model and learn time-based systems such as texts.

sator square
the sator square is a latin sentence palindrome that can be read in all directions:

S	A	T	O	R
A	R	E	P	O
T	E	N	E	T
O	P	E	R	A
R	O	T	A	S

the meaning of the sentence is disputed but an approximation could be: arepo the slave has the work of the wheel.

stop word
a stop word is a word that is irrelevant for a certain natural language processing algorithm. examples of stop words are articles and conjunctions.

text generator
a text generator is a system or a program that creates text by applying certain rules.

talespin
james meehan's talespin (1976) was one of the first text generators that could create a cohesive story without constructing it from predefined templates.

word database
in this book, the term word database describes a collection of words with additional information and links to each other. with this database, a program can, for example, easily calculate subwords or palindromes.